Spiritual War

Spiritual War

Understanding the Unseen World and How It Affects Us

Laura Van Tyne

LIGHT STREAM
FOUNDATION

Spiritual War: Understanding the Unseen World and How it Affects Us
Published by Light Stream Foundation
Oregon City, Oregon, U.S.A.

VAN TYNE, LAURA, Author
SPIRITUAL WAR
LAURA VAN TYNE

Library of Congress Control Number: 2024915777

ISBN: 979-8-9900334-0-5, 979-8-9900334-3-6 (paperback)
ISBN: 979-8-9900334-1-2, 979-8-9900334-4-3 (hardcover)
ISBN: 979-8-9900334-2-9 (digital)

BODY, MIND & SPIRIT / Healing / Prayer & Spiritual
PSYCHOLOGY / Psychotherapy / Spiritually Integrated
FAMILY & RELATIONSHIPS / Chosen Family
EDUCATION / Philosophy, Theory & Social Aspects
BODY, MIND & SPIRIT / Angels & Spirit Guides

Book Design, Cover Design and E-book formatting: Amit Dey
(amitdey2528@gmail.com)
Publishing Management: Susie Schaefer (finishthebookpublishing.com)

QUANTITY PURCHASES: Schools, companies, professional groups, clubs, and other organizations may qualify for special terms when ordering quantities of this title.
For information, email lightstreamfdn@proton.me

DEDICATION

This book is dedicated to everyone who is seeking the light
and working to create a healthy soul.

TABLE OF CONTENTS

INTRODUCTION

*M*any ancient civilizations had secret institutions called Mystery Schools. They were often secretive societies dedicated to studying God and the Universe. These teachings were passed down aurally from one generation to the next. They were founded in mysticism and spirituality, and these schools' primary focus were enlightenment, manifestation, healing, and transformation. In modern terms, we talk about light workers and healers, ascension, and other similar topics.

The concept of spirituality has been growing in popularity for a while now. For perhaps the first time in humanity's history, people seek spiritual rather than religious knowledge. Learning to take religious teachings and apply them to modern times is essential. For most of history, the church has had control over us. If we fail, if we sin, then we go to hell. If we don't pray the right way, we go to hell. If we have thoughts that are contradictory to the church, we go to hell.

Many churches guarded actual spiritual teachings, afraid to empower the people. Only religious clergy were allowed to read. Guttenberg's invention of the printing press was a game changer. People were burned at the stake for teaching commoners how to read. If the public could read, they could start creating their thoughts and opinions, gaining soul sovereignty and free will. Those in control did not want this to happen; they needed to keep their flock close.

For thousands of years, people, including royalty and clergy, depended upon soothsayers, psychics, healers, and shamans for coveted information from the unseen world.

This book was borne out of the most common questions from clients, speaking engagements, and strangers. The unseen, energetic world has always directly impacted our lives.

With the advancement of technologies, our cameras can now detect elements of the unseen world. We can see orbs, rods, ghost energies, demonic energies, angelic energies, and more.

This begs the question: How does the unseen world impact our behaviors, free will, wisdom, and insights? How can we better protect ourselves from these unseen energies? Why do we need to learn how to protect ourselves? And from what, exactly?

This book helps answer questions on a variety of topics in a logical manner, hopefully leading to new, more profound questions, observations, and learnings. We should never stop learning because knowledge is power. It's uplifting and helps us act and react with wisdom and discernment as we walk our spiritual path.

Love and blessings,
Laura

Part One

······◆······

KARMA

CHAPTER 1

··· ✦ ✦ ✦ ✦ ···

WHAT IS A SPIRITUAL AWAKENING?

A spiritual awakening is a call to your higher consciousness. What does that mean? It is simply a higher state
of awareness and understanding that helps us to have a
stronger connection to GodSource. The non-tangible senses
become more activated, such as increased intuition, an elevated awareness or perception, the ability to be mindful, or
being more present and living in the moment. It is a form of
letting go of ego.

Understand there are many ways to experience a spiritual awakening. Everyone's experiences vary and are tuned
to their specific needs on their soul's path. No person, guide,
guru, or religious clergy member will have all the answers
you seek. This is a great time to practice utilizing your intuition and wisdom in discernment. What rings true for you?
And why?

Spiritual awakenings are significant because they indicate you are gaining a greater understanding of yourself and those around you as you begin to see the universe's interconnectedness.

A spiritual awakening isn't really about unicorns and rainbows. Examining our lives through a new lens can be difficult, and our loved ones may not understand our new perceptions. It is important to remember that spiritual growth is never a competition during this process. We are where we are supposed to be.

Spiritual awakenings vary in experiences and degrees. You may begin to feel a greater sense of inner knowing. There is a shift in consciousness that enables you to have deeper connections with your soul, the world and other dimensions around you, and the Universe. These transformations do not happen overnight and vary in degrees depending on what your soul needs. A spiritual awakening can last from weeks to years, and then you may start all over again on even deeper levels.

There are many signs you may be experiencing a spiritual awakening, but they aren't one-size-fits-all. You may find that you are more sensitive to the energies of the unseen world. You may pick up on other people's emotions, and you need to realize when other people's emotions belong to them and not to you.

You may find that you are experiencing massive shifts in your perceptions and belief structures. It is also possible that your soul purpose becomes more apparent, and you begin to shift your priorities.

The 7 Stages of a Spiritual Awakening (& How to Recognize Them):

1. Increased Awareness of Your Thoughts & Emotions

   You may find that you become less reactive to the situations around you and tend to pause and react with a sense of wisdom and clarity. In meditation, it becomes easier to examine your thoughts and emotions and determine what best serves you and the greater good.

2. A Desire for Inner-Growth

   Questioning your beliefs and worldviews and how they challenge your viewpoints and values, exploring different philosophies and ideologies, and gaining a higher perspective of your place in the world. Having an open mind to accepting and challenging new thought processes may be scary and intimidating, but know that you are not alone.

3. Emotional Shifts & Heightened Feelings

   Start examining your emotions and your reactions to events around you. You start craving real connections and deeper conversations. Small talk may become annoying. Over time, you will find that your circle of friends becomes smaller yet more meaningful.

4. You Begin Noticing Meaningful Coincidences.

   Synchronicities are not only fun and enjoyable, but they also mean that you are on the correct path. You may find you look at your phone, and the time that shows up is your number, such as 11:11. It also reminds us that the universe is here for us and is listening to our needs.

5. You Can Finally Let Go of Your Ego & Self-Focus

When we let go of attachments, those self-identifying markers, such as identifying yourself by your career, your intellect, being a vegan, or even the dramas around you, are reasonable indications that your ego is beginning to diminish so that you can focus on finding your value and inner peace.

6. You Notice How Connected Everything Is

Connections come from our humanity and taking an interest in the well-being of others. It is important to note that there are two types of service: service to self and service to others. When we are in service to others, we know that we are here to help humanity and even the animal kingdom.

7. You Value Authenticity & Compassion Above All Else

You will have a more profound confidence, self-awareness, and self-worth. Being kind and forgiving to yourself for any past actions is healing to the soul. If you feel you may have caused harm and want to atone for those actions, devise a plan. Political correctness falls by the wayside.

How do you Begin Your Path toward a Spiritual Awakening? Awareness is key. Once you know, you know. Start with self-exploration. Find out what interests you and learn to understand how nature works.

It's important to remember that you are your soul. This is your journey. Looking for help and assistance when dealing with a spiritual awakening is normal, but always use your judgment and never hand your power over to anyone. Also, know that for any spiritual practitioner you seek assistance or guidance from, you have the right to ask them questions.

CHAPTER 2

······◆◆◆······

WHAT IS SHADOW WORK IN SPIRITUALITY & WHAT IS ITS PURPOSE?

*H*ave you ever asked yourself what is shadow work? The term shadow work is a spiritual buzzword people have tossed around lately. So, let's take the mystery out of it. Our shadows are those internal aspects of us that we want to avoid, deny, or even ignore. Maybe it's a fear of finances, worrying about what others think of you, or breaking negative family patterns. Or perhaps it's a past life trauma that comes to the surface, such as an odd phobia or anxiety that is not logical.

We all have parts of ourselves that we don't love or need to work on, which can change throughout our lives. When we have the courage and strength to work on these aspects of ourselves, healing, success, ascension, and so much more will happen quickly. As we learn to heal through shadow work, the dis-ease within us ceases.

Our shadows are the parts we may have rejected, buried, or hidden away. Those traumas, actions, or deeds our subconscious wants us to bury can feel too hard to deal with. The truth is that it may feel hard to heal our old hurts and traumas, but it's harder not to deal with them. These unresolved elements can hold us back.

A shadow work facilitator is a trusted spiritual practitioner or healer who can assist you in your shadow work. They may help guide you, have unique insights, and, more importantly, help you to help yourself. Whenever you hire a spiritual practitioner, ask them questions about how they can help you. Remember, you are always your soul's advocate.

A large part of shadow work is introspection. With introspection, you always need to give yourself the gift of time—the time to do the work. Meditation can be an important aspect of discovering how to listen to that small voice inside of us that offers guidance and understanding.

"There is no light without shadow and no psychic wholeness without imperfection." Carl Jung

This quote means we are not here to live perfect lives. We are here to learn and grow; after all, there is no learning in perfection. Carl Jung never thought that the shadow aspects of us were negative; they are there to learn how to shed them and to grow spiritually, mentally, and emotionally.

Our subconscious mind is often the gatekeeper to our shadow work, the record keeper of our soul's history. While it may feel heavy and looming, Shadow work is very freeing when we get on the other side. A prominent aspect of shadow work is learning to let go and understand that forgiveness has many levels.

When we are wronged, have injustices happen to us, those around us may be quick to tell you that it's time to forgive and move on with life. Easier said than done. Healing happens in degrees and waves. This is where learning to be kind and patient with ourselves is also a part of our shadow work.

There are many benefits to engaging in shadow work. When we actively engage in shadow work, it becomes empowering and raises our confidence and self-esteem. Your level of wisdom starts to increase, and you discover the ability to pause before negatively reacting.

You will notice that your relationships will improve, or you may start to let go of the unhealthy relationships. You may not be as easily triggered, especially if you have empath tendencies.

You start rediscovering your authentic self and who you are, which will feel amazing. The shedding, or letting go, feels lighter and uplifting. There is a certain level of 'spiritual' maturity that happens, and it echoes throughout all your energetic fields. You may find that others now find your personality magnetizing.

All of this encompasses a greater level of creativity and pure GodSource energies.

Shadow work enhances our self-awareness and emotional healing. We all have the power to choose our thoughts and feelings. Sometimes, those thoughts and feelings are complex to move past, especially when it comes to the death of a loved one or the shame or sadness of our actions. However, when we can move from these heavy emotions to compassion, kindness, forgiveness and understanding, we reclaim our soul healing.

Learning to be present and in the moment helps us understand what's truly important. For example, if you have a sibling who died and you find yourself at a family party thinking of him and becoming overwhelmed with grief, try to step out of it. Do something simple like wash your hands, come back, and watch the children playing or conversing with someone. This is an example of being present and in the moment.

The entire purpose of shadow work is personal, soul growth. We don't always get it right. We are here to learn. The more we know, the more we heal, and that has a substantial karmic ripple effect that echoes out.

There are many ways and strategies to do shadow work. The first step is to know what needs to be healed and to be honest with yourself. It's ok to take small steps. For example, your boss makes you nervous, and you make mistakes you would never usually make around him. Take some time to figure out why. Do you have an insecurity about authority? Does your boss remind you of an abusive parent? Figuring out what the 'why' is the first step.

Meditation and prayers are significant gifts that you can give yourself. It doesn't have to be a long time—maybe five minutes before you get out of bed. Do what works for you. The idea of spending a long weekend alone on a mountaintop isn't necessary.

Journaling and Reflective Practices can aid in shadow work. If you see a pattern within yourself that you don't like, learn to get out of the do-loop. Do you miss out on life experiences because your shyness stops you from doing what you desire? Start to write about it. What would happen if you went on that camping trip with your buddies who are expert campers? Give yourself a prompt. "I want to go camping with my friends, but I don't know anything about camping." Then free write. Go through the emotions, go through the fears. Then ask yourself, what is the reality? Chances are pretty good your friends would be thrilled to have you join them.

Through your mediation practices, learn to visualize yourself on the other side. Visualize yourself changing or interrupting your patterns. Learn to get out of your comfort zone. Shadow work takes some courage, and it isn't an instantaneous process. We need to remember we are all works in progress.

One common challenge is that we may plateau for a bit. Give yourself the time to rebalance and learn the new you. When you are ready, you may choose to continue.

When it comes to shadow work, there are some common phrases, such as 'overcoming your demons' and the like. I wouldn't say I like using the term demons in this manner. There are better word choices, such as challenges, obstacles, and hurdles. The definition of a demon is an evil spirit, an evil spirit, or a devil, especially one thought to possess a person or act as a tormentor in hell.

Shadow work is a foundational element that helps us achieve inner joy and learn how to thrive by looking below the surface. Many times, we seem to face the same blockages in life. We get to a certain point, then we plateau. A good spiritual practitioner can help you overcome those blockages and move forward on your spiritual path. See shadow work as building your spiritual armor to move forward with confidence and grace, and know you got this.

CHAPTER 3

···✦✦✦···

HOW MANY SPIRITUAL DIMENSIONS ARE THERE?

*H*ow many spiritual dimensions are there? This is the million-dollar spiritual question. The answer depends on many factors. One is your spiritual belief system and understanding of dimensions. Many religions and spiritual philosophies discuss various dimensions and break them down according to their belief structures. It doesn't make it wrong or right; it just is.

The concept of spiritual dimensions often refers to the existence beyond our physical realm and is associated with spirituality and metaphysics. There are many variations and beliefs about the idea and construct of spiritual dimensions. When I speak on this subject, I refer to dimensions where otherworldly types of beings reside.

Others categorize dimensions differently. For example, the second dimension represents the emotional realm, the third dimension is our intellect, and the fourth dimension revolves around our higher consciousness. The fifth dimension is about transcending our limitations, and the seventh dimension is pure energy.

Within Hinduism, the first dimension concerns the inside of physical objects that we cannot see, while the second dimension concerns what we can see and touch.

The bottom line is that frequencies form each spiritual dimension.

How many spiritual dimensions are there? This is a tricky question to answer properly. Some say there are seven dimensions, others say there are 27 or more dimensions, and some say there are an infinite number of dimensions and even parallel dimensions.

However, I have a definite view of the dimensions of the world where I reside and the type of work I do, which involves solving people's problems. It works for me and those I know.

Acknowledging that we live on an earthly planet where we walk around due to gravity and the Earth revolving in our planetary solar system, I realized through study and experience that my current definitions make sense.

Let's start in numeric order to not rank any one dimension in order of importance over the other. The dimensions exist and are contained by frequencies.

The first dimension consists of basic elements. Think of single-cell particles. I don't generally work in this dimension, and it's fundamental.

The second dimension is also known as the devic kingdom. This is the realm where fairies and sprites reside. They range in size from approximately 8 inches to 4 feet tall, and many have wings. These elemental beings can only utilize the energies on the planet, and humans create most of these energies. These beings work directly with nature and help to keep nature in balance.

The third dimension is where our consciousness resides. This is our physical earth plane, the dimension where time, space, and gravity combine to allow us to live out our mortal lives. This dimension is the physical everyday plane where our homes, cars, and grocery stores exist. I have a friend who says it's the boots-on-the-ground place where human tasks get completed. This dimension is our home base until we leave our physical bodies.

The fourth dimension is the place between heaven and Earth. Initially, when a human or animal dies and leaves its physical body, it goes from the third to the fourth dimension to the higher realms. The fourth dimension is supposed to be a step-up transformer to help us raise our frequency as we return Home to the higher realms. However, this dimension is now problematic.

Why? Because this is where those beings who left the light of GodSource ended up. They have hijacked this dimension, and they soul-nap human souls for their energetic benefit. They no longer have access to GodSource energy and utilize human souls. This is why it is so vital for all ghost souls to cross over to the higher realms as fast as possible.

The fifth dimension is about spiritual awakenings and the heavenly realms. When crossing over a client's loved one, I often refer to a higher dimension beyond the fourth dimension as a higher realm. The higher realm denotes a place where deities reside and is assumed to be a safe place of higher spiritual achievement.

This is also the entry point to what many refer to as the Heavens. Ideally, this is where our spiritual guides and teams, along with beneficial extraterrestrials, assist us while we live our mortal lives.

Light beings reside beyond the fifth dimension and above. They transcend time, space, and gravity and have more unity of consciousness. In these realms, there is more all-knowingness. Unlike the entities in the fourth dimension, these are the ones who abide by Spiritual Laws.

It is possible to tap into the higher realms through mediation, astral projection, or any other manner; please be wise and judicious about who, what, and where you are connecting. The dark side works hard to shapeshift and impersonate. Your soul health and wellness are the priority. One way I usually vet my guides is through the visualization technique of pouring down a high-frequency substance, such as frankincense or even salt.

Learning more about raising personal frequency is the most common way to access these other dimensions. Working with a trusted spiritual practitioner is another way to access these different realms.

The key is to build and maintain a healthy soul. Souls that are fractured, need healing, and/or don't work on themselves will find this problematic. Spirituality is not a contest; we can all work on ourselves and heal.

There is a saying that goes, "There is no such thing as no such thing." This means that we are limited by our mortal human mind construct. We can grow and heal at accelerated rates When we can open the doors with intention and wisdom and continue our spiritual learning paths.

CHAPTER 4

····◆◆◆····

WHAT IS KARMA & HOW DOES IT AFFECT OUR LIVES?

*K*arma affects all of us, whether we believe in it or not. At the most basic level, karma seeks balance. When there is tension, it's a sign that karma is out of balance, and the tension is designed to help redirect us. Karma also spans lifetimes. This is an important concept to understand. Our actions and reactions to the situations and events we encounter have a ripple effect that echoes over time, space, and dimension. The quality of our actions will influence our outcomes. Good deeds create good karma and vice versa.

We must look at karma not as punitive but as opportunities for soul growth and healing. Karma often gets bad press. We sometimes mistakenly refer to karma as revenge when we feel that someone else's acts slight us. We frequently hear someone slinging around the big "K" word: "Karma is going to get them." Or "I hope karma bites them in the booty." Karma is not positive or negative. It just is.

A karmic cycle is a spiritual learning tool through which we can master specific life lessons. These lessons and experiences are designed to help us and will be repeated until we learn what we need to know.

Karmic cycles are not negative. They may feel like that but are here to help us learn and grow. Karmic cycles are not harmful but can feel hostile, frustrating, and annoying. People often try to avoid learning these lessons because they can be rather painful. When we don't do the work to overcome a karmic cycle, we will keep receiving the same lessons over and over, and we will begin to feel stuck and hopeless. This is where we need to remember that we have free will, and the ability to change our actions or reactions to these karmic lessons is critical.

We need to remember karmic cycles are designed to help us master life lessons and to help us grow. When we are ready to do the hard work, our situations may start to change.

Life is a journey with many ups and downs and twists and turns. With this, some patterns will start to emerge and are somewhat cyclical. For example, your overbearing boss reminds you of one of your parents. What do you need to learn from this situation? Is it to learn to speak your truth?

Here Are Some Possible Signs You May Be Stuck in a Karmic Cycle:

1. You Notice Recurring Patterns & Situations in Your Life

    Look for patterns, including situations, emotional responses, and even how others react to you. These patterns can include wealth mindset, physical appearances, how we respond to dramas, and so much more.

2. You Attract the Same Kind of People Over & Over

Do you continue to date the same toxic personality? Do narcissistic people tend to find you and abuse you on some level over and over? I tend to see These couple of standard karmic cycles the most. We repeat our toxic relationships because it's what is familiar to us. This is the lesson, so we need to learn to identify and change the pattern.

3. You Are Being Forced to Face Your Fears

This is a tough one. We attract what we fear. Right now, globally, there are a lot of fears going around. If you have a fear (or more), take some time to work through it. For example, if you fear losing your job, give yourself the gift of time. Spend the time working through what that loss would entail. Work through those emotions one by one. Ask yourself what the worst thing that could happen is. And is the worst thing very probable?

Breaking free of a karmic cycle is soul-healing and elevating. So, how do we do this? Deflating as it may sound, it can take more than one lifetime. Here are some recommendations to help.

1. Spend Some Time on Self-Reflection & Awareness

Learn to identify the patterns you want to change about yourself. What is happening in your life that you would like to change? Spend time learning how you react to

situations; study the relationships you have in your life.
Learn about your relationship with finances or your career.

2. Pursue Conscious Action & Change

When we spend time reflecting on certain aspects of our
lives, we can make conscious changes. This means that we
are fully living in the present moment. We learn to look
deeply into our emotions and learn from them. This allows
us to release anxieties and fears about our situations. With
the release of anxieties and fears, change can happen.

3. Embrace Change & Forgiveness

There is a saying that the only constant in life is change.
Change is inevitable. When we become stuck in the past,
it holds back our spiritual growth. It's one thing to look
back on our memories with certain emotions, such as happiness, joy, or sadness. It's another to allow our past events
to rule and dictate our ability to move forward.

   Change often involves entering the unknown, which can
be uncomfortable or even scary. Remind yourself that all
change is simply a learning experience about how we navigate our lives. A basic concept in feng shui has helped me
embrace certain changes in my personal life: When we can let
go, it makes room for more and something new.

   If there is only one item you take away from this article,
it should be this: forgiveness is not forget-ness. All too often,
when something happens to us, those around us assign a
timetable for us to forgive a person, event, or some other
action where we have been deeply hurt or have hurt someone

else. The ability to forgive, whether forgiving oneself or someone else, is a profoundly spiritual experience that each of us owns and will navigate through on our karmic paths. There is no timeline. There is only experience and learning.

Breaking free of a karmic cycle starts and ends with you. The real question is, what do you want from life? What do you need to do to attain your goals? No one can do this for you. You are your soul. While getting help learning to identify and break patterns in your karmic cycle may be beneficial, it is still up to the individual to do the work.

CHAPTER 5

·· ◆ ◆ ◆ ◆ ··

WHAT IS KARMIC DEBT
& HOW DO YOU REPAY IT?

A hhh, the dreadful concept of incurring karmic debt and needing to repay it. This concept tends to make people fear karma or wish ill will upon those who cause harm to us. But would it surprise you to realize that karma seeks balance? Karma does not carry an emotional component with it.

We all have a cosmic ledger, a proverbial bank account of our soul's history. We may carry credits and debits. It's about balance and learning.

We all have a karmic credit score. Just like we can rack up credit card debt or create savings accounts, karmic debt is similar. A cosmic ledger is like a spiritual balance sheet, much like our monetary bank accounts. The concept of karmic debt revolves around our soul's history, where we may not have made the best decisions. As our souls move about from moment to moment, even lifetime to lifetime, we are given opportunities to make better choices, balance, and improve our karmic bank accounts. We often look at karma as a negative, impacting our outlook on how karma honestly operates.

The origin and significance of karmic debt are related to the needs of our souls. Our souls incarnate here to receive the lessons and experiences we need on our Karmic Path. Each one of us has soul purposes and missions. The theory is that we incur karma based on our actions in our current and previous lives. The concept of a karmic debt is the belief that one has carried out negative actions that have caused hurt to others, and this debt must be repaid.

Tracing the footprints of karma through reincarnation: karma has no timeline. Karma follows us throughout our lifetimes, and just as no bad deed goes unpunished, no good deed goes unnoticed. We need to remember that our souls are eternal, and these earthly moments are simply blips on our soul's RADAR.

Many times, as we look at our life patterns and where we seem to get stuck, such as addictions, sabotaging our relationships (including relationships ourselves), or even financial struggles, looking at a possible past life regression can help us unblock these karmic cycles.

Another way is to learn your karmic numbers and what they mean. Everything in the universe is about vibrational frequency, and this includes numbers. While I am not a numerology expert, there are some general basics online that are helpful to identify what your karmic numbers are based on birth name and birthdate. This is a good, basic site to learn more about your Karmic numbers and what they mean: https://www.mindbodygreen.com/articles/karmic-debt

The numerology behind karmic debt and uncovering life's lessons usually manifests as unresolved recurring issues in your life. What patterns are you looking to change? Do you find yourself dating the same narcissistic personality? Are you constantly letting others walk all over you? As an empath, do you absorb other people's energies and find yourself continually drained? There are many more scenarios like these, but the idea is to learn how to break the patterns. Once we can do this, we break out of the karmic cycle.

What do manifestations of karmic debt in daily life look like? As you look at your life and those around you, who are the people you most interact with, on either a positive or negative level? How much of your life is dedicated to managing those relationships? Are these relationships drama-filled? Or are they filled with more elevated interactions? This earth plane, our third-dimensional physical existence, is all about actions, reactions, causes, and effects. How we manage these determines our karmic debts and credits.

Karma always gives us opportunities to balance relationships. As you look at those around you, are there people in your life with whom you felt a 'love at first sight' emotion? When you met that person, you immediately clicked. Or have you ever met someone and felt "hate at first sight?" These are signs that you may have had a past life or more with them.

How do you repay the karmic debt? One of the best ways is through service to others. When we conduct our lives intending to serve others, we increase our awareness outside ourselves. When this happens, kindness, compassion, and wisdom grow within us.

Mindful actions are critical in clearing karmic debts. You may find yourself caring for an ill loved one. This could be karma playing out to balance past-life actions. Perhaps in a past life, you weren't kind to animals, and in this life, you find yourself volunteering at animal shelters. There are many ways to look at this, and we can take kind and compassionate actions to clear our karmic debts.

Embracing forgiveness to heal the karmic ledger is vital. As we work on forgiveness, we must understand that forgiveness has no timeline. The ability to forgive oneself for someone else for something done to us can take lifetimes to heal and balance. However, when we actively work on healing those hurts, we can accelerate our karma. Forgiveness can come in many forms, from atonement to learning to understand the other person's actions and where they came from. It doesn't diminish the action against us but can help in the healing process. One last element about forgiveness: forgiveness doesn't have to mean forget-ness.

We all reincarnate here for the experiences and lessons our soul needs. Living a mortal life is not easy. However, when we truly begin to learn from our surroundings and how our actions and reactions impact us and those around us. The goal is to attain wisdom and evolve as we go about our Karmic Paths.

CHAPTER 6

······ ✦ ✦ ······

WHAT IS A KARMIC SOULMATE
(& WHAT IS THEIR SIGNIFICANCE)?

*K*arma is a Sanskrit word that reveals destiny and fate. This is where we take our past soul experiences and bring them forward to help us grow and learn. The characteristics and relationship significance of karmic soulmates vary widely. The reason is that we all have unique experiences needed to achieve our soul's purposes. The relationships we have while we are here on earth are designed to help one another in many ways.

Karmic soulmates have many different characteristics based on the soul's needs. Karmic relationships can be powerful and intense, volatile and complex, and sometimes feel like home as if you have found your twin flame.

A karmic soulmate comes in many different flavors, so to speak. It may be a romantic, platonic, or even a parent-child relationship. The point is that karma knows where you need growth and assistance.

Karmic soulmates can have a strong emotional connection. We often think of the concept of love at first sight. Well, there can also be hate at first sight. I remember years ago, a good friend of mine had a sister who lived on the East Coast, and when she came to visit, this friend insisted I meet her sister. The moment I saw her, I was terrified. It wasn't logical at all. At that lunch, this sister proceeded to belittle and berate me at a luncheon. It was weird. I didn't do anything to upset her.

From that moment forward, my dreams were not my own. Something- or someone- kept entering my sleep state and haunting me. This went on for weeks. Then, one day, I went in for an acupuncture treatment, and I had a spontaneous past life recall. In this past life, I had a husband and a baby daughter. I saw that I was wearing a green dress, maybe made of velvet. In that lifetime, this woman, the sister of my old friend, strangled me to death out of a jealous rage. Karma brought us together so that I could take my power back. Once I had that past life recall, this sister never bothered me again. This was a quick and intense karmic relationship that was needed.

Children are always karmic opportunities for us. Many times, our children are also our karmic soulmates. They allow us to change negative patterns we learn from our parents or the adults around us.

Our life partners can also help us to work through our childhood traumas. Maybe we have feelings of rejection or abandonment. Perhaps we were physically abused, and we need to learn how to trust someone implicitly.

We all have life purposes that change as we grow and evolve. Soulmates offer us lessons that tend to be challenging yet rewarding. These relationships can also satisfy karmic debts or atonements for past deeds that we may not be fully cognizant of.

We are all here to learn many life lessons, ascend on our spiritual path, and evolve. Karmic soulmates are always a part of this process. The key is to be aware and mindful of our relationships and to try to put our best foot forward.

Breaking out of a karmic cycle is a big deal, including healing old wounds and traumas. Karmic cycles are a series of repetitive events, actions, or emotions. Karma wants to know if we learned the lesson. Therefore, we are always presented with the same lessons wrapped in different gift wraps. While it may not seem fair, it just is.

How do you know if you are in a karmic relationship? Look at the relationships you have had in your life. Then, ask yourself how karma tests you to see if you learned the lessons. For example, do you struggle with supervisors at work, even when you change jobs? If so, is karma offering you ways to act or react differently? What is the lesson you need to learn? Is it to listen? Is it to speak your mind? Is it learning to follow through with commitments?

Signs that you are in a karmic relationship can include a person who makes you feel insecure. Is it you, or is it the other person? There may be unexplainable synchronicities. There may be an imbalance in the relationship, such as codependency, that you need to learn to work yourself out of.

Karmic relationships are usually derived from unresolved lessons or relationships from previous lifetimes. Other types of soulmate connections help us grow, understand, and share values. They can also help support and guide us through a karmic relationship.

We are all connected and interconnected, and a relationship outside of a karmic soulmate may manifest as a more supportive person who helps you navigate difficult moments.

Navigating a karmic soulmate relationship isn't for the faint of heart. Managing all our relationships with care and love is vital to karmic growth. Our karmic soulmates may offer those lessons on a deeper level. The question we all need to ask ourselves is, what am I supposed to learn?

Learning strategies for managing intensity and conflict will help you become mindful when there is conflict, allowing you to avoid that knee-jerk reaction and eliminating regrets. When we do this, we learn and grow. If the conflicts are part of a pattern, you will need to learn how to break that pattern. When that happens, we regain another aspect of our soul sovereignty.

It's all about the lessons, growth, and spiritual ascension. Look at the patterns in your life. What needs to be changed? What can you do to grow or help a loved one to grow and learn? The possibilities are endless.

That adage, "All good things must come to an end." The same is true for the negative as well. When we learn the lessons, when that other person no longer fits our needs, or we no longer fit theirs, it can be time to move on. It's not forever. It's not necessarily a negative issue. It just is. We can learn to love that person for who they are and what they taught us.

While karmic soulmates impact our personal growth, so do all our other relationships. Again, the goal is always personal growth. When we achieve personal growth, we also attain wisdom, which helps connect us to the higher realms. It all aids in our ascension processes.

There are several types of karmic soulmates. We may have our best friend or someone we cannot live without. The one we call or talk to several times a day. Some soulmates are contentious and here to teach us lessons. We also have our life partners, maybe through marriage or another type of commitment. Then there is the twin flame, where we see the other part of ourselves within another person. All our relationships are karmic, as we are all here to learn.

CHAPTER 7

······❖❖❖······

WHAT IS A STARSEED & WHAT ARE THE DIFFERENT TYPES?

A Starseed is a person who feels a deep connection to the stars, the cosmos, and the universe. This type of person may constantly feel unexplainable homesickness. There are several types of Starseeds, each containing inherent traits and originating from specific planets or constellations. The concept of the word Starseed means that there is a 'seed' or element of that person's soul that originates from another star system, such as the Pleiades. This seed element carries within the soul light codes and other spiritual knowledge. The key is learning how to tap into this knowledge and remember.

We are all multidimensional beings. We are more than just our minds and physical bodies. We are constantly hearing about people awakening and waking up. This is often about Starseed souls who awaken to realize they have a deeper meaning or even a mission while on this planet. That element that was seeded within them is alive and growing. There is no going back once you know.

There can be many types of triggers that awaken a Starseed, such as a mystical experience of a light being coming to them, a near-death experience, or even severe harassment from the dark side, who can see a Starseed's potential future. These are just a few examples.

How can you find out if you are a Starseed? This is not intended to create a false sense of importance or hubris. Many Starseeds inherently know there is more to life than our physical existence.

When a Starseed awakens, they may find most conversations dull and mundane. They may feel that their jobs and relationships have less meaning for them. Starseeds need to learn how to cope with those feelings and how to remain engaging with those around them who are on a different frequency or path.

Signs You May Be a Starseed:

1. Empathy: A Core Starseed Trait

    Many Starseeds find themselves highly empathic. They may find that they are emotional sponges for the world around them. If they are not careful, they will allow themselves to become crippled by the energies around them and unable to function. Many times, they may turn to substance abuse and addiction to numb themselves.

    Learning to practice detached compassion is critical to empathic success. Detached compassion is the ability to separate one's emotions and well-being from other people's emotions and energies. Learning detached compassion makes us stronger and enables us to serve others better.

2. Wisdom Beyond Years: The Old Soul Aspect

As Starseeds learn to dive deeper into their soul's well-being, they will find that their levels of wisdom grow quickly. This helps us to have better actions and reactions to the dramas and situations around us. This type of personal growth allows us to live richer and fuller lives, and that energy echoes around us, ideally helping others.

Several Types of Starseeds & Brief Descriptions:
Pleiadian Starseeds: Bringers of Light and Healing
These Starseed hail from the Pleiadean star cluster. They may be the most sensitive out of the groupings. They are also highly creative, and their general goal, or mission, is to help humanity ascend.

Arcturian Starseeds: Advanced Souls with Technological Insight
Arcturians come from the Arcturus star cluster. These Starseeds have advanced technology, are analytical, and have an innate desire to learn and understand all that is around them. As children, they probably drove their parents crazy.

Sirian Starseeds: The Spiritual Warriors
They come from the Sirius Star system and tend to be leaders and protectors for not just other Sirians but all of humanity.

Andromedan Starseeds: The Adventurers and Freedom-Seekers

Andromedans are from the Andromeda galaxy. They are innovators and independent thinkers who can be rather stubborn in their thought processes. They also have a calm and steady presence in heated conflict.

Lyran Starseeds

Lyrans are connected to the Lyra star system. They can be spiritual warriors and seem to have close connections to feline entities.

Orion Starseeds: The Seekers of Truth and Wisdom

Orion Starseeds are connected to the Orion constellation. They often have a strong sense of purpose and are holders of the light to bring unity and peace to all.

Dark Starseeds

This is rarely mentioned, but there are many Starseeds of all types who are no longer on the light side. They will feign altruistic morals and principles. These dark Starseeds will create havoc and we need to know and recognize their patterns. They are great at tricking the trusting Starseeds to get their way. Many times, these dark ones work with certain dark entities. They have sold their souls to them.

All Starseeds need to understand that simply wishing and hoping does not bring the change this planet needs. We must be okay with getting our hands dirty and learn that doing actual spiritual work is never easy. Spiritual work and spiritual service come in many forms.

Many Starseeds seem to feel that certain types of work are beneath them and tend not to want to work in the third-dimensional, earth plane. That is simply not true. A waiter who serves food to others is performing a type of spiritual service. So is the person who is bagging your groceries.

Starseeds are here to assist humanity and help with the ascension of planet Earth. And that service comes in many forms.

Our beloved planet Earth and other planets are at a crossroads between the light side and the dark side. We have been watching humans commit atrocious actions against one another for millennia. My rhetorical question to you is, are those real humans committing those heinous crimes, or are they dark entities that have hijacked human souls?

Many Starseeds are considered older souls who have been around the block a few times. They may tend to be naïve, thinking that all is good and that with enough positive thinking, everything will work out. Starseeds need to have a deeper understanding of how the dark side works and what we can do to protect ourselves as we move forward.

CHAPTER 8

············◆◆◆◆◆············

WHAT IS AN INDIGO AURA & WHAT DOES IT MEAN?

*O*ur auras connect our mind, body, and soul. There are many colors, variations, and degrees of color. These colors change and flow throughout our existence, even in our daily encounters. It is even possible to have a multi-colored aura. An indigo aura is thought to have certain desired qualities of advanced spirituality.

An aura is a type of energetic forcefield. If you think back to any version of the Star Trek series, whenever the ship is under attack, someone says something like, "Captain, the shields are down 18%". And then we see the spaceship appears to be shaking and the actors rumble back and forth. Or "Captain, the shields are down to 26% and are failing". When this happens, there is some alien species invading the ship, trying to take it over, and a battle ensues. If we can use the Star Trek shields as a type of metaphor for our auric fields, it's an easier way to wrap our heads around this concept. We cannot see the shields around the ship. It is a type of unseen energy, but they can measure the strength of the forcefield.

When our auric field is strong, it keeps our mind, body, and soul in a healthier space because it is a form of protection. It acts like a barrier. For example, have you ever been so busy that when you finally get to rest, you feel like you are coming down with a cold but don't? It could be that your auric field pushed out that virus so that it could not attack your system.

Understanding the function and frequency of auras is essential to better understanding an aura and its colors. Everybody's aura is unique to them based on their experiences. When dealing with significant traumas, it may be more challenging to create a solid aura, though not impossible. The opposite is also true: When we are calm, focused, and working with intention on our spiritual path, we can learn to heal and strengthen our aura.

Do you remember having to learn this acronym in elementary school, ROY G BIV? These letters stand for the ordered color spectrum: red, orange, yellow, green, blue, indigo, and violet. Colors are light wave frequencies. All colors are variations of the three primary colors: red, green, and blue. Each wavelength (color) carries a specific frequency.

White is the combination of all the colors in the spectrum. In a sense, white light carries all the frequencies. Black is the absence of all colors and is the absence of light.

Here are the colors and what they may represent.

Red: passion, love, anger, artistic

Orange: vitality, relationships both positive and negative

Yellow: happiness, joy, playfulness

Green: love, kindness, heart-centered, compassionate

Blue: communications, intuitive, thoughtful, wise

Indigo: truth seeker, inner knowing, spiritual

Violet: artistic, creative, wise

Grey/black or muddied in color: anxiety or disconnect

Modern spiritual theory is hot on the concept of Indigo Auras. It is purported that people with an indigo aura may be more spiritual than others or that they may have more advanced psychic abilities. The truth is that all colors and frequencies are essential.

A word of caution: True spirituality is never a contest. This is where ego drives the human condition, and it can get us into some trouble. Additionally, we need to understand that our auras ebb and flow and change all the time based on our experiences and surroundings.

It is said that a person with an indigo aura generally has a deeper understanding of themselves and others. They may be less quick to judge people and situations because they understand we are all on our unique path based on the experiences we need for our soul evolution and growth.

A person with an indigo aura may have a strong sense of intuition, which leads to increased psychic abilities. They tend to have an inner wisdom in their words and choices. They may be more deliberate in their actions and less reactive in their emotional responses.

Those who have an indigo aura are thought to be on a more spiritually evolved path. These people may be referred to as an old or wise soul. You may feel you were born a light worker and have high (and realistic) expectations of yourself.

However, it should be noted that spirituality is a harmonic scale, meaning that everything ebbs and flows and goes up and down. Having said this, every aspect of us is spiritual. The difference is intention. Are we deliberately working on our spirituality? If so, ask yourself why and what is your purpose for doing so. When we become introspective and honest with ourselves, we gain the ability to see aspects and elements of our lives on a deeper level.

Developing our intuition aids in developing our psychic abilities. There are many types of psychic abilities and within each type, there are many facets and degrees. It's important to understand that these abilities are learned and earned over many lifetimes. Psychic abilities can even be taken away when we use them to cause harm or injustice.

Some choose to incarnate on this planet to help humanity and are on a spiritual mission. Not everyone has a soul mission; we must understand that we are all here for many reasons.

We all incarnate here with many soul purposes, which are wide and varied. We may want to learn how to overcome an addiction, get along with certain personality types, care for an ill loved one, and so on. These soul purposes are crucial to our soul development.

A soul mission may be someone who sees a particular element of human suffering and works to rectify it, such as creating some device that delivers affordable, clean water. It could also be someone who has an innate understanding of how the spiritual realms work and shares those thoughts and insights to help strengthen humanity.

It is possible to work on building a stronger and deeply spiritual indigo aura. Look at elements in your life and learn what is working for you and what may not be working so well and why. Meditation and prayer are also crucial moments when we seek guidance and clarity in our lives. Give yourself the gift of time, the time to spend with yourself, and getting to know yourself even better. It's those moments in the time we gift ourselves that we can take a pause and be introspective. This can be especially true after going through a trying or difficult time. Ask yourself what you learned and what would you do differently. These are the types of actions we can take to cultivate a strong and healthy aura.

CHAPTER 9

····◆◆◆····

GREEN AURA MEANING EXPLORED - EVERYTHING YOU NEED TO KNOW

What does it mean to have a green aura? Let's start with the basic premise that we all have auric fields, and our auras are frequency-based. Each color carries a frequency, and the frequency of green is between 530 and 600 THz. Auras and aura colors are more than just our personalities.

Our auras are the energies that are emitted around us. It's a part of our energetic field, the frequencies from which emanate within our fields. We need to first understand that we are all energetic beings. Our energies and frequencies change all the time. Our chakra centers also

Aura colors are frequencies, and our frequencies change all the time, depending on what is happening in our lives. Our aura colors tell us about the energies we embody or are in resonance with at certain moments in time.

Auras are indicative of moments in time. People will rarely always have the same-colored aura in their lives. If they did, it would be safe to assume they have not experienced much change in their lives. There are ways to learn how to identify what your aura color is. In addition to the technology, such as Kirlian photography, we do have the ability to learn how to see auras. People with specific psychic abilities may see other people's auras a bit more naturally, we can also learn how to see our auras using spiritual tools, such as mediation, or through intentional focus.

A green aura resonates with a variety of healing modalities. If you are familiar with the chakra system, you will know that green (and pink) are associated with the heart chakra. The heart energy is about love, personal growth, or transformation. It may also indicate one may be dealing with a lot of grief, as these are all heart emotions.

There are many degrees of green. If we go back to our childhood color charts, ROY G BIV, green is a secondary color that is a combination of yellow and blue. Therefore, the range of green is important. Does your green aura lend more to the blue side or yellow side of green?

A blue-green aura can represent harmony, balance, and calm. A yellow-green aura may represent vitality and energy.

As with all aura colors, there are pros, cons, and learning opportunities. A green aura is a heart-centered aura; it may be seeking a relationship and enjoying heartfelt conversations that have a deeper meaning. It may also tend to be a bit more serious.

The implications of a green aura are peace and serenity when it comes to psychology. Green has a calming and soothing effect on us. A person with a green aura will exude these types of qualities. They may have a 'magnetic' personality. Everyone wants to be around them.

A person who has a green aura may seek balance and feel a deeper connection to nature. They may like to be outside in nature. Walking around barefoot may feel especially good to them.

A person with a tendency towards a green aura may find themselves in professions that lend themselves to helping others, such as healthcare, teaching, or social work.

Those with a green aura will tend to be calming in their behaviors and energies around them. You may find that those with a green aura can step into a room, and everyone will immediately feel at peace. Why is this? Because energies do not have boundaries, and a green aura is one of a calming and soothing nature.

Those with a green aura may be seeking or in relationships that flow smoothly; that is especially true if their partner has a complimentary aura. A green aura will have a sense of relaxation and peace within them. This can be healing to those around them, thus improving their relationships.

When it comes to our interpersonal connections, what new growth and new relationships are we navigating? How can we attain a deeper, more spiritual understanding of what is going on around us?

All aura colors have plusses and minuses. If you are seeking to envelop a green aura, look at those elements in your life that you can cultivate to create more peace and harmony. At the same time, are there elements in your life that you need to learn to address to let go? Such as the grief of a loved one who died? Or was a job opportunity missed? Divorce? Or any other life lessons that no longer suit you?

As Kermit the Frog said, "It's not easy being green." Having a green aura often means leading with your heart. When we do that, we lead a life of vulnerability.

Each aura color carries with it benefits and opportunities. When it comes to a green aura, some of the challenges associated with this color are jealousy and resentment. If it is a super dark green/muddied color, what in your life needs to change, and why?

Balancing your green aura for optimal well-being is the goal. When karma, or life, is out of balance, there is tension. Look inside yourself to figure out what the tension is and what you can do about it. Sometimes the best we can do is simply learn to let go.

If you find you have a natural inclination for a green aura, learn about the different layers and opportunities that you have in front of you. Each color offers life lessons and spiritual opportunities as you navigate through life. Learn to embrace all that you are. We are all works in progress. We are all walking a spiritual path (even if we don't know it). But above all, learn to love yourself and those around you.

FIVE TIPS FOR RAISING YOUR VIBRATIONAL FREQUENCY

*T*he concepts of vibration and frequency have turned into spiritual buzzwords. Everything has a vibration or frequency to it. From rocks and trees to sound and light to cells and molecules, to humans and animals, planet Earth has a vibration or a frequency to it. Even our emotions have a vibration to it. Vibrations are a type of energetic rhythm and flow, the speed at which something vibrates. The real question is, what does this mean for you? Our vibrational frequency is a direct correlation to our levels of consciousness.

Your vibrational frequency is your primary state of being, how you feel, how you act, and how you respond to outside stimuli. Think about our homes, for example. Clean homes have sunshine coming through and no clutter or piles. The energy, or frequency, of that home emits a sense of peace, order, and calm. Dirty homes, shades, and blinds constantly closed and full of clutter tend to have occupants that feel chaotic, frazzled, and disorganized. These types of homes tend to have repair needs. This same concept can be applied to our physical bodies and our soul energy.

We may have been born into a family where there was excess chaos and drama, but we all can learn from our parents and those around us to learn how to do things differently. When we learn to raise our vibrational frequency, it helps us to live life with less drama and more wisdom.

Learning the tools and strategies to raise our frequency helps us in many ways. First, we need to understand that our intentions play a large part in the ability to increase our frequency.

The idea is that if we can learn tips and strategies to create a strong baseline when we get hit with something, we don't fall as hard. This means that if we have developed a naturally high frequency and we get news of a death, job loss, or any difficult issue, we can bounce back and recover quicker. We can also act and react more appropriately. A high vibrational frequency helps us grow our wisdom, discernment, and coping strategies.

When we can create a higher vibrational field, it can help keep illnesses away, as a strong vibrational field can act as a shield; think of your favorite superhero.

What frequency do humans vibrate at? The short answer is it depends on the human. We need to first understand that we are not created equal. We are created in karma, based upon our soul's experiences and the lessons and wisdom our souls are seeking in this lifetime. We all have experiences thrown at us that are unanticipated. For instance, you wake up, get ready for work, and feel wonderful. You drive to work feeling good, and then suddenly, a car swerves into your lane, almost striking you. Your emotions would change from loving and wonderful to possibly angry or fearful. Identifying emotional situations can lead us to understand more about how frequency works.

We first need to understand that our vibrational frequencies change all the time. What is helpful is to learn how to raise your baseline frequency.

"Just raise your frequency," they say. This is a frustrating answer to those who are trying to understand these concepts. We all have a first day, and no matter where you are on your spiritual path, honor that.

There are many ways in which we can do this. One is to look around your home and ask yourself, "Does this (object or room) make me feel happy or fill me with anxiety?" If your answer is the latter, what can you do about it?

Surrounding yourself with music that fills your heart and activities that bring you joy raises your vibrational frequency.

Five Tips for Raising Your Vibrational Frequency:

1. Meditation

    Mediation is listening to God or your Higher Self. Take a few moments out of your day to sit with yourself, ask questions you are seeking answers to, and then listen and feel for those answers. The answers may not come right away, but they will come. Give yourself the gift of patience.

2. Be Grateful & Practice Humility

    Gratitude is everything. We need to remember that we incarnate here for the experiences our souls need on our karmic path. Some have dealt with extreme traumas and others whose life seems to be a bed of thornless roses. Appreciate who you are, where you come from, and where you are going. At the end of each day, find three to five things you are grateful for. This spiritual practice is extremely powerful. When we can tune into our gratitude, we begin to grow on many spiritual levels.

3. Practice Forgiveness

First, forgiveness is not forgetfulness. Forgiveness does not have a timetable. When we are hurt or wronged, know that the ability to forgive may take time, and permit yourself to be kind to yourself. Suppose you have done something and are seeking forgiveness. In that case, the ability to examine what happened and come up with a plan for healing atonement not only balances out the karma but also allows for lessons learned and the ability to move forward.

4. Be Good to Your Mind & Body

Learn to spend time alone with yourself. It's an opportunity to reflect upon your situation and seek a higher source of guidance.

Examine your emotions. Take the time to analyze your feelings. Our emotions carry an energetic vibration. Emotions such as guilt, blame, and shame need to be released as best as possible. David Hawkins's book, Power Vs. Force, is a great work on emotions and the vibrational relationships within them.

5. Limit Low-Vibrational Relationships

Look around you and examine your personal and work relationships. How does a coworker make you feel? Is your boss kind and understanding or do they make you feel unworthy?

Families are the most blessed unions, or they can cause the most strife in our lives. We all have that embarrassing uncle who drinks too much on holidays or the grandma who nitpicks. We also have very loving and attentive relatives and that is who we would benefit to gravitate towards. Recognizing how these people make us feel is the first step in understanding vibrational relationships.

Learning tools and strategies to help you raise your vibration will help you grow and live your life with a deeper spiritual intent. Raising vibration also helps to heal the soul on many levels.

Part Two

· · · ✦ ✦ ✦ ✦ · · ·

SOUL HEALTH

CHAPTER 11

···✦✦✦···

WHAT IS SPIRITUAL ASCENSION?

*T*o ascend means to go up or climb. It's that simple. Spiritual ascension is about improving your soul's health and wellness. It's about the evolution of your soul and what that means for you. Spiritual ascension can also be referred to as spiritual awakening. We need to understand that each action we take, every thought we create, every aspect of us is spiritual. Our surroundings are spiritual. We cannot escape spirituality.

The concept of spirituality is not limited to only the higher dimensions or levels. Spirituality is more like a harmonic scale, with ups and downs and ebbs and flows. Many times, ascension can be a two-step forward, one-step back process. The question becomes, what have you learned from your experiences?

What causes spiritual ascension to take place? There can be many reasons. Awareness is critical to spiritual ascension. Maybe you had an experience that created an opening for you to become more aware of the truths and untruths around you. You may start questioning all types of information, from religions to the news and even your family patterns. It is ultimately the search for truth.

It seems that at this moment in history, there is a mass awakening of humanity. This mass awakening is also responsible for the divisions we see within our family structures, workplaces, and friends. Some people are moving forward at a quicker pace than others, and this may create a delta or a frequency mismatch. In this process, it's important to know that each of us is on our unique path. It is not up to us to help someone awaken spiritually if they do not ask for help or do not want help. We are all exactly where we are supposed to be. This is about the individual journey.

There are many types and forms of ascension, but these five are the ones most people have questions about. These five are chosen to illustrate the point that we are all interconnected on a microcosm to a macrocosm scale.

Five Types of Spiritual Ascension:

1. Personal Ascension

    Personal ascension is unique to you. It's the culmination of your soul's karmic path. Your actions, reactions, and the free will choices your soul has made throughout your soul's history.

    Our souls are eternal; we live many lifetimes, and our souls exist between lifetimes. When we can understand that our souls exist outside of earthly time, space, and dimension it helps to expand our conscious awareness of ascension, making ascension and de-ascension possibilities limitless.

2. Planetary Ascension

   Our planet Earth, some call it Gaia or Terra, is also involved in the ascension process, the evolution of our planet. Planets are also considered to be a life form. All life changes. This is the beauty of life as we are incarnated on this planet. We are seeing many changes; some we perceive as wonderful and others as somewhat horrifying. No planet is stagnant, and that includes our weather and climate, oceans, rivers, landmasses, and all the inhabitants.

3. Galactic Ascension

   And I am not talking about the video game, here. We are not alone. There are many, many other types of beings and entities in the universe. All beings are spiritual. Some choose to evolve or ascend; others choose the opposite.

4. Universal Ascension

   We live within the multiverse, meaning ours is not the only universe out there. Each universe is based on its frequencies and will ascend as they are ready.

5. Multidimensional Ascension

   Every dimension has specific vibrational frequencies. These frequencies create the dimensions in which a multitude of beings reside. For example, think of our color spectrum and the rainbow. Each color has its own set of frequencies, and each set looks like a layer. We can view the multitude of other dimensions in this manner, and it helps us wrap our heads around this concept.

There are many possible signs and symptoms of spiritual ascension. This is just a short list, but I know that many times, symptoms of ascension may make you feel uncomfortable. Look at them as a form of growing pains.

The questions revolve around *who I am, my purpose, and why I am here.* Begin to permeate your thoughts.

You may find your psychic abilities, especially your inner knowing and intuition, growing. Conversations with some people may begin to feel flat, as conversations about the weather are now boring.

- You may begin to feel more connected to nature and animals.
- You start to question your belief systems.
- There is a heightened awareness of the energies around you.
- You find you have a greater connectedness to GodSource.
- Your creativity is expanding.
- You have a deeper sense of inner connectivity and peace.

How long does spiritual ascension last? The answer to this is easy: How long does your soul last? Spiritual ascension ebbs and flows. Your soul may feel like you are on a huge upward trajectory for a few weeks or even years, and then it levels out for a while. While this levels out, your soul is processing all those elements of ascension, either consciously or subconsciously. Then, later down the road, you do it all over again. Look at this as a spiral staircase that keeps going up. Now and then, you get off the staircase to get to the floor you need to stop.

After a spiritual ascension, you may see the world as brighter, feel more as you go about your daily life, have your chakra system in better alignment, and have your psychic abilities naturally expand.

Spiritual ascension is a constant process, and there is no starting or stopping point. There may be periods of rest in between. I know it may sound a bit disheartening. Sometimes, I even ask myself, can I get off this merry-go-round yet?

Learning how to embrace the journey of our spiritual ascension is the golden key. Know that you are exactly where you are supposed to be. Learn to love yourself and appreciate who you are. Know that the changes you are going through are never permanent, but rather it's a part of the process.

CHAPTER 12

·· · ◆ ◆ ◆ · ··

WHAT IS SOUL RETRIEVAL & WHEN IS IT NECESSARY

*O*ne of the most common questions I hear is, what is soul retrieval? Simply put, soul retrieval is the ability to strengthen, fortify, and heal the soul. Our soul is GodSource energy. Our souls are eternal.

Christ talked about life everlasting, not death everlasting. As our souls exist throughout time, the soul energy can become broken down, fragmented, or even separated. This can happen from the traumas and abuses we experience, especially during childhood.

Soul energy is what animates throughout the physical body. When we die and leave our physical bodies, the only aspect we take with us is our soul. We can't take with us our favorite foods, our bank accounts, or our favorite piece of furniture. This is because our karmic time here on this earth is done for now. Not forever, but at least for the time being.

Soul loss can vary by degrees. Sometimes, soul loss means that there is a chronic energy leakage within the person's energy field. Sometimes, that energy leak is a small trickle. Or it may feel like the Hoover Dam has opened, and a person is left feeling chronically exhausted for no reason. You may sleep all night and wake up tired. Perhaps you never feel like you are alone, that there is always something else with you constantly tapping your energy. Another sign of soul loss may stem from constantly feeling or getting blocked in areas that deny your success.

Throughout my years of working with clients, I have seen many types and degrees of soul loss, soul fragmentation, and soul pieces among the living and the dead. Yes, soul loss can happen in death.

One of the most common ways a soul may become lost or fragmented is when a person dies and does not cross over. They don't ascend into the higher realms. They remain stuck, literally between Heaven and Earth. This is what we call ghosts or ghost energy. If there is one item I hope people take away from this, it is that every single soul needs to go Home to the Heavens and higher Realms and not linger as a ghost.

This is where the soul becomes eroded and decays the quickest. Many of our religions have taught us that bad people deserve to go to Hell, Limbo, or whatever you want to call it. If you have a loved one, or even a not so loved one who died, you have the power and ability to help them to cross over.

Living a mortal life on this planet has never been more difficult and trying than right now. We are constantly talking about and working on our physical, mental, emotional, and even financial health. But what about our soul health? This is key. The stronger we can make our soul, the smoother our lives go, and the fewer illnesses we acquire. As our strength increases, so does our ability to tap into our Higher Self and gain innate wisdom. It is pertinent that we all safeguard and protect our souls. No one can do this for you. But we all can get help and assistance. This is why soul retrieval is imperative.

When we experience childhood abuse or other traumas, it can erode our soul. It can weaken us on many levels. But this also creates a learning opportunity to learn how to treat others better, to learn self-worth and strategies on how to heal the soul.

We are seeing an alarming rate of addictions. Addictions, especially drug addictions, can shatter the soul into many pieces. When it is broken down, there are dark beings that feed off this weakened soul energy. They do this because when they left the light of GodSource, they lost their energy (food) supply.

Humans are GodSource energy for these dark beings. These dark beings are capitalizing on the human soul, working hard to break us down for their benefit. This is why addictions are so hard to overcome. An addict has dark beings that manipulate them, putting thoughts in their heads and convincing them to keep using.

When we knowingly manipulate someone for our gain, when we make false promises or derogatory accusations without merit, for instance, we compromise our soul health. This is especially true of someone who has narcissistic tendencies.

A narcissist will find someone he can manipulate to gain more power. However, this type of power is derived from the lower frequencies, the dark side. Please note that no one can change the behaviors of a narcissist. What we can do is learn to love them from a distance to ensure they do not harm us or erode our souls.

There are signs of a lost soul that you should be aware of: You may feel detached from others, or you may feel a disconnect that you cannot quite put words to, or you may feel like an outsider looking into your relationships.

You may find prayer and meditation difficult. You may find it difficult to quiet your mind, or you may see 'black' as some other solid color. When it comes to prayers and meditation, try not to overthink the process. Know that when we pray, we are speaking and connecting to GodSource and our Higher Self. When we meditate, we are listening to God-Source and our Higher Self.

There is no one correct way to pray or meditate. Do what works for you. Maybe meditation works for you when you are washing the dishes or prayer works better for you when you are gardening. Many times, we think that we need to sit in a lotus position for hours on end, waiting for some amazing message to come along. Rarely is that the case.

The inability to be in the moment and absorb the great life moments may also be a sign that your soul needs healing.

If you constantly see dark shadows out of the corner of your eye or feel that there is a negative energy or presence around you, seeking help to remove them and help with soul retrieval can be life-changing.

When is Soul Retrieval a good idea? If you are working on improving your spiritual path and seeking ways to remove blockages that are preventing you from living your ideal life, then finding a reputable practitioner to help with soul retrieval can go a long way.

What to expect after a soul retrieval? Rarely have I had a client during these sessions who failed to see an immediate shift in energy. Many times, sessions are an educational process. Sometimes, I teach clients to use time-proven tools, but almost always, there is improvement. Try it. What do you have to lose? Don't you deserve to have the healthiest and strongest soul possible?

Performing soul retrieval is an intimate process because every person is unique and has different souls and life experiences. For example, performing a soul retrieval for a person who has addiction issues may look very different than someone who sees dark entities or someone who is chronically exhausted. Finding the root cause of soul loss is key. Then, those pieces and parts can become reunited within the person. It's also critical that any spiritual practitioner who performs soul retrievals share insights on how to keep their client's soul healthy.

Do I need a shaman or other spiritual practitioner? Can I do it myself? Do I need help? How do I know? These are all great questions to ask yourself. This type of introspection can be profoundly healing. Here are some basic do-it-yourself tips you can use to assist you on your spiritual path.

Upon going to bed, and when you wake up in the morning, spend 5 minutes focusing on your breathing. Feel yourself inhale and exhale slowly. Which parts of the body are moving? Which are stationary?

Emotional Freedom Technique (EFT) is a tapping technique where you tap key acupressure points on your body to release negative emotions, and fears, and to help the energy flow through the body. To find more information, type Emotional Freedom Technique in your browser.

If you sense you have dark energies or beings around you, you can create your affirmation, such as, "I do not consent to..." or "I do not give permission for any energy or entity to harm my soul."

Also, if an issue may feel too great, you may need to consult a spiritual practitioner. We can't always do everything ourselves. Soul Retrieval is a spiritual practice that can help you heal and move forward with your life. When I work with clients on soul retrieval, they are an active part of the process. It gives people ownership of their soul health and restores their power. Soul retrieval can help you heal and move forward with your life on a deeper spiritual level.

CHAPTER 13

···◆·◆·◆··◆·◆···

WHAT IS A SOUL CONTRACT AND HOW DOES IT AFFECT YOUR LIFE?

A soul contract may have many surprising elements. Years ago, it was late Fall or early Winter when I received a message from a woman who lived in Ohio. She reached out because she found out her daughter's neighbor had a baby who died. She was concerned about this baby not crossing over. With the help of the woman who contacted me, we found the infant soul. The discussion with this baby soul was rather remarkable. This infant soul was wise beyond his six-month age. He stated his soul contract was to incarnate here to these parents in hopes of getting them back on track, so to speak. He agreed to come here to offer these parents a lesson and to allow them to make better choices.

It was hoped that when the parents found out they were pregnant, they would stop using drugs. These parents failed the test. One day, his parents were using hard drugs. While inebriated, they forgot they had left their precious little boy outside in a baby swing. The baby died from exposure that cold day. While this infant soul had only six months in his little body, his soul energy was not infantile. He came for the sole purpose of helping those parents. They had the free will to make whichever choices they wanted.

A soul contract is an agreement we make with our spirit guides. These contracts are put into place before we incarnate, before we are born, onto this planet. A soul contract involves many other people and beings. They tend to be complicated yet simple. In theory, these agreements are meant to help the person have the needed experiences for soul growth and development. We all come here to examine and experience our soul purposes. There is a myriad of soul purposes that we can explore in each lifetime.

Are our lives predetermined? The short answer to this question is yes and no. The key to the answer to the question is the concept of free will, which means we can make choices, and every choice we make does affect our soul contracts, for better or worse. However, there may be elements in our contracts that are more solid than others. For example, we may agree that our siblings join us, but based on our experiences, we may be led down a different path in our career or the place we choose to live.

Understanding what a soul is is essential to understanding a soul contract better. Simply put, the soul is the energy that animates the physical body. This energy exists beyond our mortal time, space, and dimension. We are all an energetic spiritual force that makes us who we are. We were spiritual beings far before we were human beings. Our time on this planet is relatively short when we realize our souls are eternal.

A soul contract is an agreement we make before we incarnate here on earth. It becomes a type of blueprint for your life. We can think of a soul contract as a type of outline for the mortal life we are about to live. Sometimes, the frustrating part is that these contracts tend to be under a veil so that we cannot see them. There is a reason for this. If we had all the answers, we wouldn't have these opportunities to learn and grow. It's not much different than when we were in high school, and we had to take all those final exams. We all have had the information needed, but the ability to remember and apply the information is another layer to our soul growth.

How is a soul contract formed? A soul contract is formed in a very similar fashion to any business contract. We metaphorically sit down with our guides and discuss our goals, our hopes, and desires. The plan is put into place. A part of this plan is knowing that we all have spiritual teams or guides and that we are never alone. Our spiritual team members change as we evolve or de-evolve. They are karmically earned.

I have witnessed in past life regressions some clients have experienced false contracts. These are contracts we made with impostor beings and have missing or inaccurate data.

What is the purpose and significance of a soul contract? The purpose of a soul contract is to be considered a guidebook while we live out our mortal lives. They are designed to help us to stretch and grow. They offer us the opportunities for lessons and experiences our souls need. All of us have many purposes within our souls. Sometimes, a soul's purpose is to learn how to live through childhood. For others, it may be learning to master a musical instrument. Perhaps it is also about learning how to get along with others.

There are many ways to learn how to recognize elements in your soul contract. The first is simply being aware that you have a soul contract. You may have an inner knowledge of specific people or places. You may start to realize that the difficult people in your life are teaching you lessons, and the sooner you learn and internalize those lessons, the quicker you will move forward.

Sometimes, we may have elements in our soul contract of negative patterns for which we are here to learn how to break free. Taking the time to inventory your life experiences may be critical in deciphering the elements of your soul contract. Look for clues. Does your boss seem to have the same overbearing characteristics as one of your parents? Do you seem to date the same personality type over and over? Look for possible patterns in your life. Have you learned from them? If so, have you been able to make the proper changes to improve your life and soul health?

Soul Contracts are oftentimes karmic, meaning our contracts span our soul's history and seek balance. If we lived several lives as an unscrupulous businessperson where we took advantage of others, our soul contract might be to have the experiences of other people taking advantage of us so that we get a deeper understanding as to the havoc we may have caused others.

When it comes to navigating and fulfilling our contracts, we need to understand that our contracts are about developing our souls and expanding our knowledge through mortal experiences. When we complete one or several elements of our contract, new elements and opportunities may open for us.

We can renegotiate and release soul contracts not for our benefit or the greater good. We have free will and authority over ourselves to do so.

If you sense that you have a harmful soul contract, you have the power within your soul to change that. This will take a lot of introspection, exploration, and studying. It may also require the assistance of a trusted spiritual practitioner to help you navigate through your contract.

Taking time for yourself through meditation and prayer may be extremely helpful. Look back through your life and examine those uncomfortable parts. What did you learn? How have those lessons helped you?

We all have soul contracts. If you are seeking more information about your soul contract, a past life regression or contact with your Higher Self may give you the answers you are seeking. Spiritual work is just that. It is work, and it will pay off. Don't you deserve to have the healthiest soul possible?

CHAPTER 14

····◆◆◆····

HOW TO REPROGRAM YOUR SUBCONSCIOUS MIND & EMBRACE SPIRITUAL TRANSFORMATION

What Is Subconscious Reprogramming? Our subconscious mind is responsible for many elements of our soul health. It is responsible for our successes and struggles. The good news is that we can actively reprogram our subconscious mind to free ourselves to live a richer and more full life.

Do you feel you are blocked or stuck in life? Do you feed your frustrations and end up sabotaging your success over and over? Why do we do this to ourselves, and what can we do to change our outcomes? The solution lies within our subconscious mind, and we should learn how to reprogram our subconscious to break through those barriers.

The first question we need to ask ourselves is, what is the subconscious mind? How is it different than our conscious mind?

Our conscious mind is where our wishes and desires come from, our emotional reactions to situations, and our awareness of self and our surroundings. This is also where our egos reside. Many times, our conscious self may not accurately recall events that happened because the ego gets in the way. The conscious mind is more about the now what is happening in the moment and what decisions need to be made for an optimal outcome.

Our subconscious mind is another aspect of our soul's being that assists us in many ways. It has a homeostatic impulse, which controls our breathing and regulates our body functions and temperature. It's what continually keeps us alive.

Understanding the connection between the subconscious and spiritual growth will help in spiritual evolution. The key is using our conscious self to positively influence our subconscious thoughts to learn how to undo or reprogram the negative patterns we are trying to break free of. This is a powerful tool that will aid us in our spiritual growth and the ascension process.

Our subconscious mind also has a huge impact on our spiritual well-being. On a spiritual level, our subconscious influences our creativity and inspiration and is also the record keeper of our soul's history. Subconscious memory is virtually perfect because it is connected to the Akashic records, which are the records of your soul's history and all universal events.

When we undergo a past life regression, either spontaneously or through a more formal setting, it is the ability to access the subconscious memories that can help us remove irrational fears and other blockages that prevent us from living out our true potential.

The first step is to learn to recognize what is holding us back and why. Where did we learn those patterns? Did they serve us well in the past? Is it time to move forward?

Our limited belief systems often begin in childhood. This is a form of programming that we all experience, no matter how wonderful or traumatic our childhood may be. We need to remember that, in most cases, our parents did the best job they could raise us based on their belief structures. Having said that, our souls may have needed certain experiences, and as we evolve, those experiences and thought patterns no longer serve us. If you have a sugar addiction, look at what elements of your childhood may have lacked the "sweetness" in life. When we can learn to acknowledge those feelings, we can begin to reprogram our subconscious mind so that we are not lacking.

Religious upbringings can potentially be responsible for limiting our belief systems. These become ingrained within our subconscious at an early age. This is mostly due to religions trying to control their masses. Guilt, blame, and shame are constant themes in most religions. These three emotions are low frequency, and often, we create forms of self-punishment, which lends itself to a sense of lack.

Past life issues are another common element that may hold us back from achieving our true potential. When we engage in a past life regression, our subconscious and higher self come forward to help us get the answers we seek. Our higher self works with our subconscious self to decide which information is most pertinent to our unique situations. Our subconscious mind, through regressions, can help unravel and reprogram our minds to free us from what is holding us back.

Unearthing subconscious blocks is hard work that pays off in high dividends. One strategy is to review our life patterns, events, actions, and reactions to what happened to us. When we do this, we also work through the emotions that can hold us back.

Positive self-talk affirmations create a subtle, energetic shift. It's important to know that we can create our affirmations and tailor them to our specific needs. Not to mention, when we create our affirmations, it empowers us. Many times, the negative programming we have received was designed to take away our power.

Journaling is a great first step in learning how to reprogram our subconscious minds. Spend the time writing down your lifetime memories, the positive and the negative. How did this experience make you feel? What did you learn from it? How often do you have these feelings? If you find fears creep in while journaling, write down the worst-case scenario and ask yourself how likely this will happen. Chances are good, but not very likely.

I also recommend writing with pen and paper. When we are physically writing, we can feel much more profound than when using a computer with electronic interferences. Pen-to-paper allows us to have more concentrated thoughts for longer periods. Not to mention, if you find yourself crying heavily, you won't damage your computer.

Visualizations and guided meditation are powerful strategies for reprogramming our subconscious minds. However, starting may be difficult. Our subconscious minds may want to hold on tightly to the concepts of "lack." It's a protective mechanism and a very limiting one at that. For this reason, journaling may be a good first step.

Vision boards are another helpful aspect of visualization. Do you need another, more reliable car? Maybe you're missing a vacation. Find photos and make a collage. Be sure to look at it each day, especially before you go to bed. This is the last thought you have before you go to sleep.

What is exciting is we can use our conscious minds to reprogram our subconscious minds. When we learn to do this, we can harness our new superpower of positive thinking to overcome negative thoughts and bad habits to achieve all our life dreams. We all have the power within us to do just that.

As we work with our subconscious self, we also set intentions and make connections with our higher self. The more we can connect with our higher self, the more we become in touch with GodSource energies.

As we learn to work with our conscious and subconscious minds, we are expanding our consciousness and awareness. This is what spirituality is all about.

Reprogramming our subconscious minds to break free of negative thoughts and patterns is soul healing. We must remember that we all can do this. For some, it is easier than others, but that is ok. Remember, we are all on our karmic path of soul healing and soul evolution. Don't you deserve to have the healthiest soul possible?

CHAPTER 15

···◆◆◆···

WHAT IS SOUL FRAGMENTATION
& WHAT CAUSES IT?

S oul fragmentation damages the person's energetic field, the soul essence. There are many reasons why a soul may become fragmented, split, or have pieces missing. Most common are unhealed traumas from our current or even past lives.

Soul fragmentation also happens because of the unseen energetic world around us, from low vibrational frequencies to negative entities wreaking havoc upon us. Fragments are pieces to the whole. We can collect and heal those fragments. This will strengthen our souls, and as we do so, we gain knowledge from those experiences and healings.

When we are robbed of our free will, experience painful traumas, and have no boundaries with others- allowing them to walk all over us, our soul health breaks down. It needs to be healed and restored. This applies to our past lives, as well.

Soul fragmentation happens when pieces of your soul separate and dislocate. A part of your energy field is off, lost, or even stolen. In many of my videos, I discuss the concept of soul napping, which is the result of the unseen dark entities harming us; many times, we don't even know it's happening. We feel off, depressed, angry, weepy, and we are not sure why.

The concept of soul fragmentation was discussed in ancient Greece through the works of Plato. "False words are not only evil in themselves, but they infect the soul with evil." When there is evil within the soul, it breaks down the soul's health.

As mentioned earlier, there are many potential causes of soul fragmentation. When we can learn to identify the trauma or cracks in our foundation, that is the first step in healing. Give yourself the gift of time. The time to allow yourself to feel the hurts, figure out what is not working well in your life, and what you can do about it. After all, you own your soul.

The negative impact of soul fragmentation varies greatly, especially when the person refuses to address certain behaviors and afflictions. Narcissism, sociopathy, and addictions are some examples of people who are existing with fragmented souls.

I would be remiss if I didn't mention the unseen, energetic external factors impacting our soul health, such as possession or mind-control elements from these dark entities. The most crucial factor in healing these souls is the ability to properly remove them and any implants or devices, heal and restore the injured aspects of the soul, and even perform actual soul retrievals. Many dark entities are in pursuit of the human soul. We need to be aware of this and be proactive.

Emotional and psychological effects impact our soul health. Facing the fears. Many of us have experienced childhood traumas. These traumas, many times, happen because, as a child, we do not have self-governing authority, and those adults in charge may be abusive emotionally, physically, and mentally. When we experience traumas, it stunts our growth. As we heal and learn from those events, we can move forward with a certain level of forgiveness and understanding. Many times, this type of soul healing is referred to as shadow work.

There can be physical symptoms linked to soul fragmentation. Not always, but those who are chronically ill, never feel well, or something may always be off are dealing with physical symptoms of soul fragmentation. This is due to the constant and chronic loss of energy in their energy field. Learning how to heal this type of soul fragmentation and the ability to stop the energy leaks goes a long way to improving our physical health and any needed medical treatment.

The opposite of soul fragmentation is soul retrieval. We all can heal our souls. There are many ways to go about it, and a lot depends on what you feel is the most important aspect to focus on.

A shaman is someone who claims to have access to entities and spirits that exist outside of our physical realm. Shaman seems to be more of a buzzword lately, and anyone can take an online course to claim that they are a shaman. Shamans do not own the market when it comes to soul retrieval. Many times, when we think of the concept of soul retrieval, we hear the word "Shaman." Just because a practitioner has the title shaman, to them, does not make them all-knowing,

a guru, or anything else. If you decide to work with a shaman, ask them how they do their practice. A red flag is if they
need to use mind-altering drugs to connect to the spirits in the
unseen world. If they do, how do they know they are beneficial? After all, they are in an inebriated state.

Knowing that YOU oversee your soul—no one else is
important. While we may need help and seek out a spiritual
practitioner, always ask them questions. If you don't like
what is happening, it's worth it to speak up and even leave if
you feel you may be harmed.

Nature is soul healing. Many parts of nature emit negative ions, which is healing. Negative ions are molecules that
float in the atmosphere (air) and are charged with electricity. UV light (sunshine), pine trees, salt water, and even thun-
der and lightning emit negative ions. Negative ions increase
levels of mood-enhancing serotonin, helping to relieve stress
and anxiety and boost our energy. While you are in nature,
spend some time in meditation and prayer; you may find that
extremely healing. Make being in nature one of your spiritual
practices.

Many energetic healing modalities are being made available to us. The trick is to find what works for you and why.
Reiki is one of these healing modalities. However, if you seek
our healing through reiki, ask your practitioner how they
clear themselves between clients and how they identify and
remove negative attachments or dark entities.

Past-life regression is another technique that can be used
for soul retrieval and healing. Acupuncture, qi gong, and
reflexology are other available energy healing techniques.

The more we work on creating a healthy and vital soul, the more resilient we become when we come up against difficult times. Maintaining a healthy soul takes consistent effort, a willingness to learn new strategies and techniques, and to consistently work on raising your frequency.

CHAPTER 16

··· ◆ ◆ ◆ ··

WHAT IS SPIRITUAL BYPASSING, AND WHY IS IT DANGEROUS?

Spiritual bypassing happens when we use spiritual concepts to sidestep authentic healing. One way this happens is when we create a false sense of enlightenment, which harms the soul.

Spiritual bypassing occurs when we use spiritual practices to compensate for true soul healing and restoration. Some signs of spiritual bypassing include using spiritual practices and teachings to cover up issues such as low self-esteem, financial ramifications, constant and chronic relationship problems, and not dealing with fears. Our egos play a large part in spiritual bypassing.

Spiritual bypassing is also a defense mechanism that creates a false sense of truth so we don't deal with our problems, and then we can blame others for the way we conduct our lives.

The term was first coined by a transpersonal psychotherapist named John Welwood in his book _Toward a Psychology of Awakening_. According to Welwood, spiritual bypassing is using spiritual ideas and practices to avoid facing unresolved emotional issues, psychological wounds, and other traumas.

Spiritual bypassing is harmful to the soul. One of the negative side effects of spiritual bypassing is that we deny ourselves the authentic self-love and compassion we need to resolve our issues and heal. This form of defense mechanism we put into place creates a wall that separates us from our emotions.

It's important to note that when we avoid healing the traumas in our lives, we will carry them over into our future lives. This means that our traumas and dramas build up within our soul energy over and over until we properly heal and deal with them. It also can mean that we reincarnate with pieces of our soul missing, and we need to work on retrieving those soul elements. Doing the hard work now pays off for an eternity.

Spiritual bypassing is a superficial element that allows us to gloss over our problems to make us feel better in the short term, but nothing gets resolved, and problems continue to manifest.

There are many signs of spiritual bypassing. The following are just a few examples.

- Not allowing yourself to be angry because you believe spiritual people don't get angry because anger is a low-vibration emotion.
- Believing that you are spiritually superior to others.

- Creating high or unattainable ideals of idealism.
- Feelings of detachment that you don't belong in here.
- Insisting this is your last incarnation on this planet.
- Focusing only on spirituality and not being in the present.
- Being overly optimistic in all aspects of life.
- Projecting your negative feelings onto others.
- Pretending that things are fine when they're not.
- Thinking that you can overcome your problems with just positive thinking and not doing the hard work.

Recognizing spiritual bypassing in ourselves and others gives us a sense of inner wisdom to change our reactions to situations.

Recently, I have seen a common form of spiritual bypassing: people using their spirituality to compete with others. Spirituality should never be a competition. "I am more spiritually advanced than so and so." We need to learn to respect and honor where someone is on their spiritual path. If we were all the same, we would be robots, right?

People who have narcissistic tendencies are excellent at spiritual bypassing. They tend to tell you what you should be thinking and what you should be doing. Their focus is on others rather than themselves. They also are not interested in another person's healing and soul growth.

People who purport that they are spiritually advanced insist that all is happy and positive with the world, and if you are not, then you are lesser of a person.

Meditation and mindfulness are important skills to develop as we embark on our spiritual paths. When we meditate, we become centered and listen to our Higher-Self and our spiritual teams for guidance and assistance.

We can develop mindfulness through our meditation practices; they go hand in hand. When we walk a path of mindfulness, we learn to be more present in our minds and lives when we can take in and absorb our experiences without judgment.

Learning to be authentic in our actions and reactions is critical to avoiding spiritual bypassing. It takes practice, and we need to give ourselves the gift of time to pray, meditate, and become more mindful of our actions.

When we learn to feel, we heal. It's that simple. We need to learn how to use our emotions as we continue our spiritual journey. The key is to realize if our behaviors indicate spiritual bypassing patterns. Ask yourself how you conduct your life and impact others around you.

If you don't feel, you can't heal. It's that simple.

The ability to practice detached compassion is an important aspect of developing our wisdom and spiritual intellect. Detached compassion means that we can be of service to others. We can understand and empathize with someone's painful situation, but we have the wisdom not to absorb their feelings.

CHAPTER 17

$\cdots\leftarrow\diamond\rightarrow\cdots$

DOES EVERYONE HAVE A PAST LIFE: UNDERSTANDING REINCARNATION

*O*ur souls are eternal, which means we all have past lives and have reincarnated. Christ spoke of life everlasting, not death everlasting. The truth is, we have all lived many lifetimes on this planet and possibly other planets. Our souls also exist in the realms of our 'in-between' lives.

Reincarnation is when the soul returns to the physical plane of existence into a new body. It's said we choose our body types and parents and come in with karmic contracts to help our soul have experiences and lessons to elevate us to the next level(s). Sometimes, some choose to reincarnate to help with a mission of helping the planet or humanity.

When we explore past lives, we consider that we have lived a mortal life before this lifetime. Past lives can offer us cues and clues as to who we are as soul energy.

I would ascertain that we all have lived past lives. Perhaps the question should be, have we all lived past lives on planet Earth?

"I am never reincarnating here again." I have heard this from many people. The reality is we are multidimensional beings. This means we have higher selves, spiritual teams, and other higher-dimensional beings that assist us. This is a 'group' decision.

"I was Cleopatra," or some other high priestess, king, etc.... Most people have reincarnated here over and over as farmers or workers. Have you also ever noticed no one ever claims to have been Eve? lol

There is a lot of evidence and case studies around reincarnation. I have done many past-life regressions (PLRs), and I am always astounded by the process and findings. When I do a PLR, I am often fortunate enough to see what my client sees, which helps with findings in these non-tangible areas.

I have had clients who were from other planets, dimensions, and so on. I can never anticipate what will be discovered, nor would I want to.

I remember walking into an Eastern Imports store in Hillcrest, San Diego, with one of my daughters. She was eight years old and begged me to go in with her. Once we were in, the shopkeeper said hello to us. That is when she walked up to a statue of Kwon Yen and said who she was and how she lived a lifetime with her. Then, she went on to talk about another lifetime in Tibet, where she would carry water on her shoulders to her village. The detail she went into was incredible. Then she became very homesick for another time, another place, and was sobbing. She said those were good lives. There is no way anyone or I could have told her about those elements. This was a spontaneous past-life recall.

During a PLR, I remember one client saying, "I was a very bad man." I was thinking, whoa, this will be interesting. My client, in his current life, is 40 years old and a drug addict. He started taking drugs when he was 14 years old. His first dealer was an African American kid in high school. He finally became clean after decades of hard drug use. He wanted to do a PLR to find some answers and to help him gain the confidence to never return to drug use.

During this PLR, it was discovered that in his most recent past life, he was a drug dealer in Chicago, Al Capone era (he currently resides in another country). In this life, he sold drugs to inner-city African-American kids. He made so much money that he had a wife and two children who lived in a country mansion and a nice flat in Chicago with a mistress.

Was this lifetime karma showing him the damage he caused and giving him the opportunity for atonement?

What are some of the signs you have experienced a past life? Look around you. What are you drawn to? What are your likes or dislikes? Have you ever met someone who you felt was love at first sight? Or hate at first sight? Those can be clues as to your past lives.

A past-life regression may also help solve the mysteries of unexplained fears and phobias. People fear heights, doctors, snakes, and on and on. If I were a betting person, I would say it has to do with past life experiences and traumas. Our subconscious remembers everything that has happened to our soul, and sometimes, these not-so-irrational traumas are more rational than we give credit.

Déjà vu is the feeling that you have done something before you have experienced it. Somehow, an old memory was activated. However, déjà vu can stem from many factors, from past lives to alternate timelines to different dimensions.

Have you ever been driving in a new area and somehow knew exactly where to turn? Or did you meet someone and know them instantly? These could be déjà vu or old memories popping up.

There are many ways to uncover your past lives. You can hire a professional. You can also try to find out information on your own. You can also start to analyze your dreams. Do you have recurring dreams of specific situations that feel intensely familiar and may or may not feel connected to your current life?

To try to learn on your own, you can work on setting intentions during meditation. "Which past life is most affecting my current life?" With this intention and focus, you may do a series of mediations (no time limit or minimum) to find clues. You may want to keep a journal of your thoughts and discoveries.

When working with a past life regression therapist, ask them questions that you need answers to. Please don't allow them to push you around. This is about you and your soul health.

Make sure the person you choose to help you is healthy, not compromised, and feels right for you. Ask them questions. Please get to know their philosophies a bit and do your research. Make sure the practitioner doesn't ask leading questions, which may skew your results.

It is said that we, on average, reincarnate here approximately every 150 years. We live mortal lives for the experiences we need on our karmic paths. Everything we do is spiritual because we are spiritual beings. Period. Every lifetime is significant.

The goal for any PLR should be to come across information that can help you understand negative patterns, heal from past traumas, and remove blockages for success.

Many times, after a PLR, clients will tell me they feel more complete and at ease, and unexplained anxieties have been released. They have a sense of peace and release of irrational fears.

Learning how to remove or see through the past life veil can offer us insights into living a life with more healing, security, and understanding. Past lives are always a curiosity. I do advise that no one should tell you what they think your past life may be. That well-meaning person could be wrong! Instead, work with a PLR therapist who is certified. Ask for credentials. I have studied and hold credentials in a couple of different techniques. Remember, you are your soul. And don't you deserve the best?

CHAPTER 18

···✦✦✦···

WHAT ARE THE BENEFITS OF
A PAST LIFE REGRESSION?

*T*here are many benefits to a past-life regression for someone actively seeking a deeper understanding of their
soul's history. Our souls are eternal. Sometimes, someone
says, "They are an old soul." This usually indicates a person
who utilizes wisdom and discernment over an emotional
knee-jerk reaction to a situation.

What is a past life, and do we all have one or more? Everyone has past lives, and we have all lived many lifetimes. Many
religions know this. Yet, some religions have taken the concept of past lives, or reincarnation, out of their religious texts
to gain more control over their "flock." Let's face it: if you
have one chance to 'get it right,' you will follow the orders
of the religious clergy in hopes of attaining access to those
pearly gates upon death.

The truth is we get many chances to "get it right." We all reincarnate to this planet for the experiences and lessons our soul needs. This planet is rich in those opportunities.

Past life regression therapy is a tool that we can use to find information about some of our past lives. During a regression, what will usually happen is the person is presented with the past life that is most impacting their current life. This can be very helpful when trying to understand some of the more difficult personalities in our lives. It may also help in understanding why someone may have certain physical or mental difficulties, as they are often left-over energetic signatures from past life traumas. Clearing these energies can be extremely helpful.

Past life regression therapy entails that the practitioner works with the client to put them in a theta state of relaxation so that their subconscious and Higher Self can come through. Our subconscious is the recorder of our soul's history and can work with our Higher Self to determine what revelations are needed to best help the soul.

When I do a regression, I send my client a list of questions to help focus the session. We then spend a decent amount of time going over that person's history, including what they are hoping to gain from a session. I remember a specific mom who wanted a past life regression to find out why all three of her children had different handicaps- from seizures to heart surgery to autism. She wanted to know what she did to deserve this. The answers were very humbling. Her children needed these experiences for their souls' learning. These children picked this mom because she was the one they felt could best help them. At the same time, the mom had agreed to have these children in her life to help them.

Some people have spontaneous past-life recalls. These can show up as a form of déjà vu, or maybe you have an affinity to a particular culture, quickly pick up a foreign language, or get triggered by an irrational fear of water. Look at your life, see what resonates with you, and start putting some puzzle pieces together.

There are many benefits to past life regressions. One is an increase in self-awareness. Perhaps you have been dealing with a fear of heights. Then, during a past life regression, you discovered you were pushed off a building or mountain. While this may sound scary, a competent regressionist will walk you through those traumas in a safe manner. As you go through this past life recall, the muscle memory of the soul is healed, and you may find that you are no longer afraid of heights or that the fear is now manageable.

A past life regression may help you to understand your soul's unique history and experiences, which allows you to gain insights and awareness of your everyday happenings. You begin to make these 'aha' connections. For example, suppose you had a parent who was tyrannical and overbearing, and now as an adult. In that case, if you find that you have a boss with these same personality traits, you can look at your situation with a lens of discernment and can react with more wisdom to certain situations. Once we learn the patterns, it can be easier to overcome them.

Another benefit is the ability to heal from physical, emotional, and psychological traumas. When we do a past life regression, it is common for our Higher Self to revisit the past life that most impacts our current life. I had a session with a public speaker client, and suddenly, she became afraid to go out in public. When we did the regression, she discovered that she was a sheriff who was shot in the stomach at an event in the 1800's. After that 'aha' moment, she has been fine, and I love seeing her out in public doing her thing and fully confident. Once the awareness is made, the wound from a past life trauma is greatly diminished and may even fully disappear into a distant memory.

A past life regression offers us a lot of introspection as to why we act or react in certain ways. If you find you often go to a place of fear or doom and gloom, it is worth investigating why this is for you.

Many times, there may be people in our lives that trigger us easily. A past life regression can help strengthen your connection to a Higher-Self to gain more autonomy and understanding of how to react with a heightened sense of wisdom to manage negative emotions and feelings. Learning what may emotionally trigger you and why is a powerful soul lesson that you will carry within you. This knowledge is very powerful for your greater good.

If you find the right practitioner, you may also be able to work on healing certain physical body ailments and develop conscious control over your whole body. You become more in tune with your subconscious, conscious, and Higher-Self. It's a form of recalibration, so to speak. A past life regression meditation involves the ability to quiet the mind and personal space.

Can anyone be regressed? The short answer is yes; however, some people may require more time to get to the theta state, which is fine. It is essential to know that your Higher Self will ensure that you are fully protected while you are in the theta state. The practitioner cannot do anything you do not consent to. I once had a young man who wanted to do a regression but was concerned he would embarrass himself.

If you are seeking a professional past-life regression, it is essential to do your homework. Make sure the person is trustworthy and has experience helping others in this manner. Ask them questions you may have before you commit to a session with them. If you feel uncomfortable or don't like their answers, that person is not a good fit for you. And that is ok because this is about you and your soul healing.

CHAPTER 19

·· · + ♦ + · ··

TEN SIGNS OF REINCARNATION TO HELP YOU CONNECT WITH YOUR PAST LIFE

*O*ur souls are eternal. Christ speaks of live everlasting, not death everlasting. We reincarnate here for the experiences. There are religions that have taken this concept out of their doctrines to gain control over us. For example, they may tell us we have one chance to get it right: to do the right things, or else our souls will burn in an eternal hell. That is not how the system works, and these fear-based types of religions are designed to control and manipulate the masses. It's also not true that when we die, we float up to a cloud and play the harp for eternity. The truth is we have many chances to live and learn and evolve and grow. We also get to reincarnate within our soul or family groups.

Everyone will experience reincarnation as we are all here for the experiences we need. We have some control over every incarnation we experience. For example, we will reincarnate here in different colored bodies, different cultures, and languages. When it comes to elements of racism, we need to truly understand we have all come here in a variety of colors. Is it possible that a "white" man who came to the United States and murdered Native Americans and then returned as a Native American? To learn what life is like as a Native American? Or vice versa? We are seeing so much division in society based on color and belief systems. What if we start to look at these human elements with an eye of wisdom and discernment? What if we look at them from a point of view of humanity? How would that heal the wounds that so many feel are inflicted upon them?

It is very possible to learn about one or more of your past lives. One of the easiest ways is to look around and see what or who feels familiar or like home. What type of artwork interests you? Are there certain parts of the world that you feel an affinity for? Certain foods you love or hate? These can all be clues to parts of your past. There are many ways in which we can learn about our past lives.

Ten Common Ways to Gain Insights Into Our Soul's History:

1. Past-life memories and vivid recollections.

   You may have a spontaneous past-life recall, feel like you are in a new location or meeting someone, and feel an unexplained sense of familiarity. You may also have realistic visions or dreams.

2. Unlearned skills and talents displayed from an early age.

There are people who seem to be born with a certain sense of knowing. At a young age, you learn how to fix cars, play an instrument, or develop any other skill set without formal training. These could be clues to bits of your past life history.

3. Phobias or fears linked to past-life traumas.

Any irrational fear or phobia could be a clue, such as a fear of water. Could it be that the person had drowned? When we can confront that fear or phobia through a past life regression, it often disappears.

4. Repeated dreams or visions of past life experiences.

If you have repeated dreams or visions, it could be your psychic muscle memory coming through. People who have died in wars may find this happening to them.

5. Birthmarks or physical anomalies corresponding to past-life injuries.

Birthmarks and other physical anomalies can be clues. A port wine-colored skin discoloration could have meant that the person died in a fire. A dark brown stain could indicate someone died of a bullet, sword, or arrow. These marks on the body are a form of muscle memory.

6. Recognizing familiar faces from past lives in current life.

Is it love at first sight or hate at first sight? We reincarnate with people we have been with in the past. Have you ever hugged someone you just met, and they felt so familiar? Why is that? Perhaps your souls see this more as a reunion rather than an initial meeting. Or have you ever met someone that just repulsed you? There could be a deeper reason for that.

7. Strong attraction or aversion to certain cultures, languages, or traditions

    If you find you can't get enough of a certain culture, or maybe you learn a foreign language quite easily, this could be a sign of a past life recall. Or are there certain foods you loathe? Take some time to meditate and explore those aspects and see if you can come up with more clues.

8. Sudden changes in behavior or preferences without apparent cause.

    Sometimes, when we reach a particular age, we might experience an unexplainable change. For example, maybe at the age of 25 in your previous life, you became the leader of your tribe and took that responsibility seriously. Then, in this lifetime, around the age of 25, you change direction and become more serious about your lifestyle.

9. Feeling like an "old soul" or having wisdom beyond one's years.

    Do you sometimes have an inner knowing of a situation? Or perhaps, as a young child, did you know more than the adults around you?

10. Intense and unexplainable emotional connections to certain places or historical periods.

If you see or go to some event or historical location or read about a place or time and you become extremely emotional about it, chances are pretty good that you have some connection that may be unexplainable to the logical brain. Perhaps there is more to the story than you know.

Connecting with your past lives begins with you. Connecting with your past lives can help you in many ways. If you are interested in exploring your past lives, there are many avenues in which you can explore.

You are your soul. You have a deep and long history with your soul. When we learn to connect the dots of that history, it can help us move forward with deliberate wisdom and an inner sense of knowing.

CHAPTER 20

···•◆•···

KARMA AND REINCARNATION: HOW DO THEY AFFECT EACH OTHER?

Warning: The relationship between karma and reincarnation is wound tightly together, but perhaps not in the way we have been taught. This is not going to be the average lofty book on the subject. As with all information, take in what rings true for you and evaluate your why.

*O*ur souls are eternal and each of us incurs karma and we all do reincarnate over and over. Whether or not we want to believe it or not. To make this a bit more complicated, we also need to consider not all souls reincarnate from the higher realms. Not all souls reincarnate fully intact. We hear of the concept of soul retrievals all the time. This is not a new concept but an opportunity to put some pieces of the puzzle together.

Exploring the relationship between karma and reincarnation is fascinating. I have spent a lot of my lifetime learning about and removing the dark entities that wreak havoc on us. These entities reside in the unseen, energetic world, and they affect us in negative ways without our knowledge or consent. We need to learn to identify when thoughts are not our own or when our actions and reactions are out of character for us. This is where the power of prayer and meditation can help us understand if there are any unseen entities or energies affecting us.

GodSource gifted humanity with the concept of free will. This means we can think and make choices based on our situation or circumstances. However, when we are being "puppeted" by these nefarious unseen entities, they unwittingly strip us of our full free will. Many people have what I call "mitigated free will." This means that we may not be fully in control of our thoughts and actions. Yet, at the same time, we are always karmically responsible for our actions. It's not fair, but it is up to each of us to work hard to understand how our actions impact others and to learn how to break those negative or harmful patterns.

We need to learn how to take our power back. It is up to us to recognize those elements that are not ours and say no more. To state that you do NOT consent. This is the basis for understanding we are in control of our soul's health and wellness.

Karma and reincarnation depend upon each other. How many times have we said to ourselves, "If I had to do it over again, I would…." Well, my friends, we do get to have do-overs. And each one is a karmic opportunity. Positive behaviors and actions create positive karma. The more generous and positive karma we incur, the healthier our souls become, and it will impact our reincarnation cycle. Karma seeks balance.

Newton's Third Law of Motion states that "For every action, there is an opposite and equal reaction." Newton has it right. Karma is always in motion. Karma is never stagnant or still.

Everything we do will have an effect. This karmic ripple effect echoes out over time, space, and even dimension. For example, if a person died in a car accident and that soul did not cross over and is stuck at that point in time at that accident scene. A year later, another driver (3rd dimension) who may be sensitive to energies sees that ghost energy (4th dimension) out of the corner of their eye and gets into a car accident, which is an example of how karma transcends dimension. This is one of many reasons why every single ghost soul needs to cross over to go Home. You can find the tools to help them in this book, Soul Tribe: Navigating the Spiritual War.

Karma is universal, yet the dark side, the negative unseen entities feel that they are entitled to work outside of the basic tenets of karma and Spiritual Law. This is not true and when I work with clients and remove those entities, they are always surprised. If you feel you have an entity attachment, you must break free, and they are properly removed and returned to GodSource.

We all reincarnate with karma attached to us. Some people come in with a cute designer handbag of karma; others come in with a freight train of karma. We are all different and unique.

We are also responsible for our actions and reactions. As individuals, our actions and reactions will ripple out. Think about water for a moment. When you throw a pebble into the water, the small rings echo out over the water, going farther and farther. This can be thought of as a karmic ripple effect. But what happens when someone throws a large rock or even a boulder into that water? The smaller ripples become over-ridden within the ripples of the larger rock. Think about that person you know who is always throwing around their energies. Those energies affect us all. We all know of at least one of these people. They can be considered a karmic test. What are you learning from them?

There are many forms of karma: family, location, group, and even planetary.

We are born into families based on our karma and the experiences we need with other souls. Each family is a school-house of knowledge and experiences. We often reincarnate with the same soul group, and we play different roles within each reincarnation. Perhaps in this lifetime, your current mom is now a cousin. The souls are the same, but the relationships are different and offer us different perspectives.

Perhaps in a previous lifetime, you were responsible for removing the native people from their lands, causing harm and disruption. Now, in this lifetime, you live on the same land where the conditions are harsh. You are now experiencing the consequences of your previous life actions.

Locations are also karmically earned. Locations are interesting as this is a form of group karma. Groups of people come together for many reasons, experiences, and opportunities.

The main principle of reincarnation is that our souls are eternal. Christ spoke of life everlasting, not death everlasting.

Many religions and philosophies speak about reincarnation, the fact that we are reborn to live a mortal life over and over.

Our lives and lifetimes are interconnected—our past, present, and future lives. Reincarnation is ideal for our soul's growth and knowledge. Each time we reincarnate on this planet, we are offered a myriad of opportunities to learn and evolve.

Let's talk about skin color. It is a taboo subject for many, but would it surprise you to know that we have all reincarnated in various skin colors, ethnicities, religions, and ideologies? This is an important concept. More people have died in the name of God than for any other reason. The truth is that we get to experience many religions within all our reincarnation cycles. We also get to experience living with a variety of different body types, including gender, skin color, shapes, and sizes.

One common belief is that we need to suffer to incur more positive karma. I firmly believe these thoughts are derived from the dark side. In most of my work, I am assisting people to free themselves from dark entities. These dark ones mitigate our free will and hijack our choices. This does impact our karma, but we are also responsible for our actions and reactions no matter the

Karma does have an impact on all our lifetimes, past, present, and future. When it comes to our future lives, the karma that we are incurring in our present life and in our previous lives will impact our reincarnation cycle. The actions we take now will impact our future lives. There are elements of karma that are not satisfied in one lifetime. Sometimes, we need several lifetimes of getting hit over the head by the cosmic 2x4 to learn the lesson. This is okay; we are all on our own karmic paths and timetables.

Honestly, if the entire world believed in reincarnation, I think we would have a much better planet. If any of the bad actors out there could spiritually understand the havoc they are wreaking and the negative karmic load they are incurring, they may make better choices. In fact, their spiritual teams may begin to change for the better. Our job is to learn how to navigate our lives for the greater good.

Identifying our patterns and learning how to break those patterns will help us to break free of negative karma. This also lends itself to creating more positive karma to accrue in our karmic bank accounts.

The more we learn, study, and grow, the more aware we become. This means we live and heal our souls with intention and discernment. It's not always easy, but those bumps in the road are excellent opportunities. This is especially true for those who have endured endless abuse. Abuse teaches us what not to do; sometimes, those are the most exquisite lessons.

I often hear from people "this is my last lifetime on this planet." That is not up to us to decide. It is up to Karma and the Lords of Karma to work with you and assist in those decisions. If we can look at reincarnation as an opportunity to learn and grow, and if we can look at reincarnation as a service to others and to better humanity and the planet, this is fully embracing our soul.

Learning about our past lives can help us to understand many difficult aspects of our lives and learn how to make different choices for the betterment of our souls.

CHAPTER 21

···✦✦✦···

DOES EVERYONE HAVE A TWIN FLAME, AND WHAT ARE THEY?

*T*here is a common question within many spiritual communities regarding whether everyone has a twin flame and how one can find one's twin flame. The concept of a twin flame is someone who mirrors one's soul, personality, and emotions. Some purport that twin flames are two people who share the same soul. When these two people come together, the relationship may seem intense and move fast.

Are Twin Flames Real? This is the million-dollar question. Regarding any aspect of your soul's health, you need to ask yourself if this ring is true for you. Follow that up with a why or why not.

A twin flame is simply a deep soul connection we may have with someone. This type of relationship can be challenging and frustrating, but learning how to handle those challenges can also be healing.

Sometimes, those challenges may be the ability to work through the problems mutually; other times, it may be knowing when to leave if those challenges cannot be rectified. For example, if one of you has a substance or other abuse issue that the person is not willing to put the effort into to heal. That is not your problem to solve for them.

Twin flames are also there to help one another achieve their goals in life. Although they may have different careers or interests, they have an innate understanding of one another's goals.

Not everyone has a twin flame. The twin flame concept is real, but not necessarily for everyone. It depends upon what your soul needs or is seeking. Some people enter this incarnation with a contract to find their twin flame; others may not have this element within their soul contracts as they have different soul purposes.

I would be remiss if I didn't mention that one doesn't need to pay a service to find their twin flame. Always be wary of any form of a psychic who can tell you who your twin flame or life love is for a fee. I say this because what if that spiritual advisor is wrong, and you end up seeking out a completely different person than who was intended for you? A spiritual practitioner can guide you and help you to attain wisdom and discernment, but the real work is still yours to do. To do otherwise is a form of spiritual bypassing.

When you meet someone, there may be an intense sense of recognition and a feeling of knowing that person before, a sort of love at first sight. There is a strong sense of yearning for that person when separated from one another. Remember that the concept of love at first sight, is not necessarily romantic love.

Twin flames offer spiritual and soul growth potential as we learn from each other. Ideally, your twin flame will challenge you to do better and heal old traumas from your current and past lives. You and your twin flame may have similar soul purposes or perhaps a soul mission.

Many times, when we come across a person in our lives, chances are pretty good that we have known that person from previous lifetimes. If you find you have a strong emotional reaction to a new person in your life, that is a sign. By a strong emotional reaction, it could be love at first sight or even hate or fear at first sight. Your subconscious is the record keeper of your soul's memories.

We are here to learn about our souls as we embark upon our spiritual paths. As we meet and interact with others, we are afforded opportunities to grow. If you come across someone who you feel is your twin flame, you are being afforded the opportunity to learn from one another.

CHAPTER 22

·· · ◆ ◆ ◆ ·· ·

HOW TO CLEANSE YOUR SOUL (7 SPIRITUAL DETOX TIPS)

*H*ow do you cleanse your soul, and why is this a thing? To answer the first question, yes, we do have a soul. The ability to cleanse our soul goes back to soul healing and restoration. Let's face it: Living a mortal life isn't easy. When we create rituals, habits, and other spiritual practices designed to connect our mind, body, and soul, we strengthen and heal the soul.

What we are talking about here is a spiritual detox or cleansing. That adage, cleanliness is next to Godliness, means something. We are multidimensional beings, and the ability to learn how to clean and clear ourselves is important to our soul's health. Our minds, bodies, and souls process and take in many frequencies and elements. With a spiritual detox, we get the opportunity to remove negative patterns, thoughts, and ideas that do not serve our greater good.

What does it mean to cleanse your soul? Just like eating well, exercising, and cleaning your home, cleansing the soul is not much different. It's a bit more esoteric and not quite as tangible as eating a good salad. However, when we cleanse the soul, we work to remove negative emotions and behaviors and examine our relationships. This allows us to allow space for newer, higher-frequency energies to come.

It's essential to prepare your mind and environment for a spiritual cleanse.

Remove all, or as much as you can, electronic devices. Our beloved phones, computers, iPads, etc.… are all embedded with erratic energies that do impact us, even though we cannot see those energies. Create a calm and quiet space for yourself. While we all have different living situations, small children, roommates, or whatever your situation, we all need a space that is our own, even if it is in our car, with the sunshine pouring in. A quiet space helps to center the mind.

By creating a sacred space, you are giving yourself the gift of time—the time to meditate, reflect, heal, and grow. Be creative, and fill your sacred space with items that bring you joy.

Meditation gives us clarity and focus when we decide we need a spiritual detoxification. It affords us the opportunity to let go of who we are and focus on where we are going and how to get there. This is a crucial component of spiritual ascension. The ability to clear our minds and let our thoughts flow can be difficult at times. If this is you, work on meditation for 2-3 minutes and then move on. This is not a contest. It's about where we are; some days are easier than others.

There are many ways to cleanse the soul. The following are a few ideas that you may find helpful.

How to Cleanse Your Soul (7 Tips):

1. Setting Intentions for Spiritual Clarity

   When we set intentions for spiritual clarity, we are, in a sense, seeking knowledge and enlightenment. Make a habit of setting an intention for a goal you are seeking. Is your intention to quiet the mind? It could be to hear from your spirit guide while meditating. We are all unique in what we need and expect from ourselves.

2. Embracing Solitude for Deep Reflection

   Learn to love spending time with yourself. Do something for yourself, even by yourself. Suppose it is hard for you to go out alone for dinner, a hike, or a cup of coffee. Investigate why that is. What can you learn from spending time with yourself?

3. Using Nature as a Catalyst for Spiritual Renewal

   Nature is GodSource energy. When we get out in nature, we become exposed to natural detoxification elements, such as negative ions from seawater or even pine trees. Get outside and breathe deeply. Go on hikes. Stop and meditate. Do what feels right for you.

4. Fasting to Rejuvenate the Mind and Spirit

   We expend a lot of energy digesting our foods. Mainly if the foods are processed carbs. There is a lot of information out there regarding intermittent fasting. Intermittent fasting can help us gain clarity and even feel more energized.

5. Engaging in Mindful Meditation Daily

Mantras and affirmations have been used to help us focus and overcome obstacles, enhance our clarity, and keep our thoughts more positive. The best ones are the ones you create for yourself. They can be as simple as, "I release all negative energies from my mind, body, and soul right now."

6. Cleansing with Ritual Baths and Their Significance

Why is it that we get our best ideas in the shower? It's because water helps us to connect to our subconscious. Epsom salt baths are a great way to cleanse and detox. Epsom salts, magnesium sulfate, is a mineral compound that helps muscles relax and calm the nerves; when added to warm water, it absorbs through the skin more efficiently. If you have serious skin ailments or infections, please consult your doctor first. How much Epsom salt is needed? On average, one to two cups per bath. You can also add some of your favorite essential oils.

7. Utilizing Crystals for Energy Clearing

There are many crystals you can use. All crystals carry piezoelectric qualities that help us clear them. It's also important to remember to clear our crystals consistently. Sunlight is more powerful than the moonlight. The moon is a satellite that reflects the sunlight. Except for amethyst, rose quartz, and a few others will fade from the sunlight. You can also bury them in the soil to absorb negative energies or put them in salt.

Maintaining a cleansed soul is similar to showering daily. We need to make it a habit. It doesn't need to be a massive production or a long list of rituals. Keeping it simple gives us more success.

Daily prayer and meditation are the most accessible and practical spiritual health practices. Exercise such as yoga or hiking helps to rebalance our chakras and clears our minds. Keeping a journal, spending time doing something you enjoy, or volunteering are great ways to maintain a healthy soul.

These are all spiritual practices. That means we need to do them—practice. Reflecting on our spiritual actions gives us the opportunity to analyze what is working and what is not working. What works for one person may not work for you, and that is okay. After all, we aren't robots, and we are not one-size-fits-all.

Assessing your spiritual health and growth after any spiritual clearing or healing is essential. We consider all aspects of our daily lives, from jobs to mechanical issues to relationships, but spiritual health should be paramount. Enjoy the journey, respect yourself, and evaluate what you have learned.

CHAPTER 23

···✦✦✦···

SOUL SOVEREIGNTY: EMBRACING YOUR SPIRITUAL AUTONOMY

*S*oul sovereignty is crucial to our spiritual autonomy. When we strive for spiritual autonomy, we also advance spiritually, which helps us improve our lives by freeing ourselves of negative energies and even dark entities.

Soul sovereignty is about spiritual freedom and free will. We must understand that achieving soul sovereignty has many facets, layers, and aspects. One important aspect is that GodSource has gifted humanity free will. This means we can make choices based on the circumstances and situations around us. Each choice we make has a ripple effect that echoes out to those around us, whether we know it or not. The same holds for actions we receive from others.

We all have spiritual autonomy. When we make free will choices, we are allowed to learn from our decisions. This enables us to grow and develop on many levels. Making wise decisions with the information at hand affords us true spiritual autonomy. We are often bombarded with outside influences that will affect our free will and spiritual autonomy. The key is to learn to recognize when we are being influenced and learn what to do about it.

When we begin to embrace our soul sovereignty, we begin to tap into our personal power. We begin to break free from the chains that bind us. Wisdom, inner knowing, and self-guidance become easier, and so does connect to our spirit guides and other higher-dimensional beings.

When we attain soul sovereignty, we claim our path, our decisions, and our well-being and walk forward with intention and discernment. When we are guided by our intuition, we create our own journeys and experiences. We are now in control of mastering what we want to learn. Is it financial freedom? Success in relationships? Learning new skill sets? The opportunities are endless.

As we learn to improve and enhance our soul sovereignty, we gain access to knowledge from the higher realms. This is a learning process. The connections we create with our higher selves allow us to grow stronger and stronger.

We need to recognize that we are all spiritual souls that have existed throughout time, space, and dimension. We are eternal. We are multidimensional. We are always a work in progress.

Some Tips to Regain Your Spiritual Autonomy:

1. Recognizing Your Inner Power

   We are not here to live perfect lives. We are here to learn and experience what life is like in a mortal body. If our

lives were perfect, there would be no learning opportunities. There are no perfect parents, perfect children, perfect
bosses. You get the idea. Once we can begin to recognize
what we have learned and how we have grown, we take
back our power.

2. Practicing Mindfulness and Meditation

One of the best, most powerful gifts we can give ourselves
is time. When we gift ourselves the time to be mindful- the
ability to be present and in the moment, we get to experience life a bit more fully. For example, you are hosting a
family reunion. It's easy to rush around, ensuring everything is perfect and that everyone is having a wonderful
time. But do you give yourself permission to stand back,
observe, and feel the joy you created for others? Do you
allow yourself to participate in the activities, or are you
too busy taking pictures or texting? Life nowadays is
extremely fast-paced. Being mindful brings us back to our
soul energy.

Mediation is another important soul sovereignty gift we
all need to give ourselves. When we meditate, we slow
down and listen to ourselves, our spiritual teams, and
GodSource. Here is where we get the information and
knowledge we are seeking to

3. Setting Boundaries

Failing to set boundaries is, perhaps, one of the most detrimental actions we can take to attain soul sovereignty.
Failing to set boundaries is a form of self-harm. There
are degrees to which the boundaries may be reached. For

example, if your boss is constantly asking you to take on more and more without compensation for time off or bonuses, you begin to be his doormat, so to speak. This is a form of self-neglect and harm. It's up to each of us to learn how to set appropriate boundaries. Not only will it help us, but it will also help those around us.

The most significant common challenge in embracing soul sovereignty is to understand that progress, all progress, is a big deal. Our souls reap the benefits whenever we make changes and improve our situations.

Soul sovereignty means we no longer need to rely on external sources for confirmation or making decisions. Our soul already knows the answer. We can vet or test the answers to ensure we are on the right track. This form of inner knowing may ebb and flow as we learn self-mastery in this area.

Self-doubt is often based on our self-esteem. We all have come here with some self-doubt in various areas, and that is part of our learning curve. This is one area where our mind and our personality come into play. Self-doubt is one aspect that is a basic element of being human and learning how to rise above—self-doubt ties into our egos. A healthy ego means we are assured of our decisions. For example, I would want my surgeon to have a healthy ego in his practice. This same surgeon may have to work on other interpersonal self-doubts, such as family balance.

There are many tools we can use to help us along our way regarding soul sovereignty and spiritual autonomy. Learning to utilize our intuition is one of our most powerful tools.

When you come across a pattern or blockage, write down what it is. This is your prompt. Write down your thoughts, emotions, situations, and other encounters from there. Start to look for patterns. You can meditate and reflect on your circumstances. As you do this, you will find new answers and abilities to release what no longer serves you.

Rituals and ceremonies help us create consistency and patterns in our mortal lives. They also help us connect to the Higher Self and GodSource energies. It's important to note that if any rituals or ceremonies leave you feeling in a good space, you have not compromised yourself in any way.

True soul autonomy may feel like a bowl of alphabet soup. All the letters and words are there, but they are all mixed up. Learning how to sort the letters to make sense of it all is a puzzle. But it's a puzzle worth working on toward completion.

Part Three

· · · ✦ · · ·

DARK ENTITIES

CHAPTER 24

......◆◆◆......

WHAT IS THE LOWER ASTRAL PLANE, AND WHAT IS ITS SIGNIFICANCE?

*T*he lower astral plane is also known as the hells, limbo, purgatory, or the fourth dimension and can go by many other names. It is significant because it is a lower vibrational plane, or dimension, of existence. It wasn't always supposed to be this way, but through a series of events over millennia, it shifted.

The lower astral is a heavy-density plane where ghosts and dark entities reside. Why would a ghost co-mingle with dark entities? When a person dies and does not cross over into the higher realms, they literally get stuck in hell, between Heaven and Earth.

It is said that the lower astral is divided into three parts: high, middle, and low. Each one is denser than the previous one. I have seen more than these three levels. I have witnessed "pocket dimensions" many times. These dimensions are usually created by dark entities trying to hide within the lower astral.

The lower astral should not be what it is. The lower astral is the 4th dimension. This is the place that all holy texts write about to give us mortals guidance for ascension once we die and leave our physical bodies. In the Bible, it is the 23rd Psalm. "Yea, though I walk through the valley of the shadow of death, I will fear no evil, For You are with me; Your rod and Your staff, they comfort me. This is our guidance to get out of this dimension.

Contrary to popular belief, Jesus did not come to the earth plane to die on the cross to absolve us of our sins in perpetuity. If we really think about it, not only does this make no sense, but it's frankly simplistic. What if Christ came here to mitigate the damage caused by the Lucifer Rebellion? What if Christ and the higher-dimensional beings realized that the Luciferic forces hijacked the fourth dimension and that this was their way of helping us and guiding us out of the lower astral?

The lower astral is cold, dark, and full of dark entities. It is full of caverns and home to all sorts of dark entities. The stuff of which nightmares are made. It's our duty for our souls to help other souls escape this nightmare, and we can! This is where knowledge is power. If we know what is there, bypassing is quite simple. We need to start educating ourselves on what to do upon death.

The vibrational energies and frequencies are very dense and low. When I help the dead to cross over to the higher realms, many times, it's as if they are in a deep, dark, dense, cold bank of fog—the type of fog where you can't see your hand in front of your face. There is a deep cold there. Many people who can sense ghost energies will say they felt they were walking through a cold sensation for a moment. This is because ghosts are cold to the bone but without the bones, of course.

I work in these dimensions pretty much every day. In this space, there are all sorts of dark beings and entities, from reptilians, greys, lower realm entities, standard black magicians, the hat man, and so much more.

It's important to note that there is a political hierarchy in every dimension and organization. For example, the lower realm entities, these harasser beings, serve black magicians. Their job is to extract our energies and give them to their bosses. If they fail, they are punished severely.

The greys and the reptilians work independently from each other and sometimes together. They reside in the fourth dimension, but they can manifest into the physical, as well. Each type of being and entity is unique to their species.

Have you ever heard the saying that bad things happen to good people? Well, this concept also applies to the lower astral plane, meaning these dark entities work to capture human souls. Why? When they left the light of GodSource, they realized they needed an energy source. Humans are GodSource energy. They figured this one out quickly.

This information is not intended to scare but to provide valuable knowledge. Remember, once we know, we know. The lesson is that we have died and reincarnated many times. We need to remember how to get Home once we leave our physical bodies. There is never any form of soul restoration or healing in the lower astral. It's our job to help ourselves to remember how to cross over to the higher realms.

It's also a substantial spiritual service to help other ghost souls cross over and go Home. We all have the power within us to do this. Request a team of angels from the higher realms to send all ghost souls interfering in your space right now.

There are many forms of shadow aspects. Oftentimes, it is referred to as egotism, laziness, and these types of behaviors. When dealing with the lower astral, there are often shadow aspects or pieces or parts of the soul that get damaged. These pieces can be retrieved and healed. We need to know that this is so. There are many shamans and other spiritual practitioners who help with soul retrievals. Soul retrieval is just that. It is bringing together parts of the soul to the over soul for healing.

There are many ways in which the lower astral influences us on the Earth plane. This usually happens on some psychic level. We are all psychic. Psychic abilities come in all sorts of flavors and degrees. For example, some people can see the dead; others may feel their presence or have an inner sense of knowing that something is amiss. This is a great opportunity to learn to trust your instincts and your intuition.

There are many forms of spiritual protection that we can employ. It's our responsibility to learn what works for each of us. It is not my or anyone else's responsibility to ensure you are protected. We can ask for help and guidance, but it is up to the individual soul to do its work.

The bottom line is that everything is math, and everything is frequency. When we learn to look at the different dimensions or planes, we can see how they are separated, like layers on a cake. That frosting area between the cake layers is where the dimensions can overlap. This is how the 3rd and 4th dimensions can interconnect.

The lower astral plane is a busy place and can be full of traps and other nefarious activities. However, as we learn how to raise our vibrations and understand how these planes of existence operate, we will regain our soul sovereignty. The Karmic Path courses are designed to help you help yourself.

CHAPTER 25

···+ ◆ +···

WHAT IS A PSYCHIC ATTACK?

A psychic attack is an invasion of any aspect of your soul: the mental, physical, and emotional bodies that make us who we are by another entity or even a living person. Psychic attacks can be caused by nefarious unseen beings or entities, low energy or frequency fields, and even living people can be the source of a psychic attack.

A psychic attack is an unseen energetic force that is trying to steal or manipulate your energy field to break down your soul. In the spiritual realms, we often hear the concept "as above, so below." Attacks happen all the time in our physical world. We hear of robberies, rapes, murders, and everything in between. The same is true in the other dimensions, primarily coming from the 4th dimension. What makes these types of attacks difficult is that they are coming from the unseen realms, and we need to work on tuning in to see what is happening and why.

Everything is energy, and energy does not have boundaries. When it comes to psychic phenomena, we need to understand that they are simply a form of energy. Many people are sensitive to this type of energy, and each person's sensitivity is unique. Sometimes, it's a "gut feeling," or you may see something out of the corner of your eye or physically feel or hear some element that is unexplainable to others. Learn to trust your intuition.

Like many physical attacks in our mortal world, the same concept should be applied to psychic or spiritual attacks. Throughout our planet's history, every era, culture, country, and language contains concepts of angels, demons, and even ghosts. If this were not true, how could it be?

One of the most common misconceptions about psychic attack symptoms is being told, "It's all in your head." Or a child being told they have an overactive imagination. Not only are these concepts dangerous, as they give the dark side more power because we are told not to trust our instincts, but they also harm our souls on many levels. If you feel or are wondering if you are under some psychic attack, it's worth exploring your signs and symptoms. Keeping a journal of the events and your feelings will help you to discover negative patterns. You can also add what actions you took to help yourself.

Identifying the Unseen: Five Signs of Psychic Attack:

1. Emotional Turmoil

    Do you find that you are easily upset by 'nothing'? You may find that you take someone else's words or actions the wrong way, misreading their intent.

2. Unexplained Fatigue

Do you consistently wake up exhausted for no reason? If so, there may be some entity or energy draining your energy field. You can take some steps to mitigate and even stop this type of psychic attack. One important aspect is to learn how to raise the frequency of your home and living space.

3. Nightmares and Sleep Disruptions

Nightmares and night terrors are not normal. If you have a child who is experiencing this, chances are those (including doctors) will tell you this is a normal part of childhood. I am going to be blunt: no form of terror is normal. Those around us will try to tell you this is a normal part of life because they cannot come up with a 'logical' explanation. There are many ways to protect yourself and your children in the sleep state. One way is to request angels from the higher realms to come in and protect you and your loved ones.

4. Recurring Negative Thoughts

Most recurring negative thoughts are not ours. These are derived from the unseen entities that are trying to wreak havoc upon us. I remember a client I worked with recently who kept having such thoughts. We worked to remove the entities, and then a month later, she told me her suicidal thoughts had stopped, never to return.

5. Physical Ailments without Apparent Cause

Ah, those medical mysteries. One of the most common physical ailments I see is this low-key chronic and non-productive cough. You aren't sick, or if you were in the past, it was months ago, and a persistent cough keeps you up at night, making your ribs ache. It's exhausting. Chances are this is likely a psychic attack. One remedy is to get 100% pure frankincense essential oil, and you can dilute it with a carrier oil of your choice to make it last longer. Put it on your chest, neck, third eye, and crown chakra. This essential oil has a very high frequency that creates a barrier and heals.

Not all psychic attacks are the same, and not all remedies will be the same. Begin by looking for the cause, the leak, or the entry point. Who are the people in your life? How are you conducting your life? Start asking yourself some hard questions to get some answers. Ask GodSource and your angels for help.

The bottom line is frequency. The higher we can raise our frequency, the less likely these attacks will happen.

Being mindful of your situation is essential. Take some time to figure out when this happened and what was going on in your life then. Prayer and positive affirmations are also beneficial, especially from the heart. In the book Soul Tribe: Navigating the Spiritual War, there is a prayer to remove dark entities that many have found helpful.

It's not uncommon to seek professional help with psychic attacks. If you do, ask and do your homework. There are many excellent and not-so-wonderful practitioners out there. Doesn't your soul deserve the best possible outcome?

CHAPTER 26

···✦✦✦···

HOW TO SHIELD YOURSELF FROM
NEGATIVE ENERGY FORCES

*L*earning how to shield yourself, your living spaces, and your property against negative energy forces is good hygiene. This goes back to the saying, "Cleanliness is next to Godliness." Part of learning to shield ourselves from negative energies is learning how to raise our frequencies, as this creates a stronger baseline for us to deflect negativity.

Negative energy can come from many aspects of our lives, including low-frequency locations. Have you ever driven to a new location and felt creeped out, as if you couldn't get out fast enough? There is a reason for that. There is a part of you, maybe your Higher Self, that knows something and is trying to warn you to get out.

Negative habits and addictions such as drug, alcohol, or even sugar addictions lower our frequencies and make it more difficult to keep our frequencies high. Many times, there are unseen entities that overshadow your willpower to ensure your addictions. Learning to take your power back and to be kind to yourself in the process is key to success.

Negative people can also impact us. Maybe it's a loved one who is an energy vampire or someone with chaotic energy that leaves you drained after spending a short amount of time with them. Someone with anger issues, a victim personality, or even a chronic complainer. When it comes to people, look at them as learning opportunities. How can you learn to act or react differently to make sure their negativity doesn't stick to you?

Once you know, you know. It can be that easy. Once you learn how to recognize and understand how negative energy works and affects you, the quicker you can clean yourself up. This is where a strong intuition can help us. Learn to 'feel' the air around you. When you go into a meeting or a family reunion, how does the energy feel? Is it joyous and happy, or is the tension so intense that you think you can cut it with a knife? Learn to discern the energies around you.

The first strategy for protecting yourself from negative energy is consistency. When we feel like we are being bombarded, it can be difficult to be consistent. This is when having someone close to us who understands these concepts can be helpful.

Establishing and maintaining personal boundaries is key to success. This is especially true when it comes to sensitive people and empaths. Negative entities love empath energies because they are easy to access. Learn to keep your power. When we allow others to take our power or abuse us, not only does the offender earn negative karma, but we can, too, especially if we allow those patterns to repeat or continue.

The Oxford Dictionary defines self-awareness as "conscious knowledge of one's character, feelings, motives and desires." As our self-awareness increases, it becomes easier to detect and deflect negative energies, entities, and influences that are around us. Give yourself the gift of time to explore how to improve your self-awareness.

Many of these techniques are visualization techniques. The mind is our most powerful asset. We all can create and manifest using our minds and willpower. This can be used for the greater good or not. And this is, again, where karma plays out. The point is, be true to yourself.

Visualization is a powerful tool for creating an energy barrier.

The power of white light. White light is a tool that spiritual practitioners have used for millennia. You will hear people say to surround yourself in a bubble of white light or surround yourself with white light. While this sounds good, we need to remember that energy has no boundaries. So, how do you keep this up to keep yourself protected? Use another visualization technique: place yourself, your home, and your minor children inside a tetrahedron and fill that with white light. Why a tetrahedron? Geometrically speaking, this is one of the strongest and simplest shapes we have. Let's face it: bubbles are easy to pop.

Christ consciousness, or Universal Consciousness, when paired with the white light, can create a powerful form of protection.

Self-talk and the use of positive affirmations help to remind us that we do reside within our power. If you have a difficult time with a family member who tends to upset and displace you, the next time you see or speak with that person, come up with an affirmation ahead of time to help you keep your power.

Creating a positive environment is key, but it's more than just creating a positive environment. It's also about spiritually cleaning your house. The ability to remove what doesn't work for you, change your negative habits, and increase self-awareness is paramount. Many purport to be highly evolved spiritually but fail to do that hard work. I call this Spiritual Bypassing, and this fools no one except the person who pretends to be highly evolved.

Know that you are in this for the long haul, and there will be bumps in the road. Continual learning is key. Everything evolves, including negative entities and energies. Nothing in our universe is stagnant. Creating and learning new strategies helps to create that shield we are looking for added spiritual protection. There are many visualization techniques, but sometimes we need physical objects to help us as well. Years ago, I spent tens of thousands of dollars trying to figure out what could help me and my family. I find that scaler technologies can be the most helpful. There are many types out there. Do your research and find what works for you.

Finding those who are of like mind is essential. We need to know that we are never alone. Even if no one in your inner circle understands you at this level, start to meditate and pray that you will find those helpful people. It may take some time, but make the time and be specific about what you are seeking. The Universe and our angels are with us.

Negative entities thrive in areas of negative energies or low vibrations. It's a part of everyday life, and there are also learning opportunities. Remember that every day is a new opportunity to learn something new to help you on your spiritual path.

CHAPTER 27

· · · ✦ ✦ · · ·

WHAT IS HEAVY ENERGY & HOW DOES IT AFFECT US?

*H*eavy energy can be considered a heavy etheric weight that can hold us down, exhaust us, and even create a loss of productivity. Have you ever heard the expression, "The tension was so thick you could cut it with a knife?" This is a classic example of heavy energy.

Everything has a frequency and energetic signature. Many energy workers understand this. Energy workers can mitigate and transmute negative and heavy energies so they can be properly removed from their clients and/or properties. Energy is simply frequency. Many types of frequencies are constantly bombarding us. When these energies are low vibrational, they feel heavy and overwhelming.

- Common Sources and Causes of Heavy Energy
- Chronically negative people

- Negative emotions
- Dirty electricity
- Electromagnetic frequencies
- Unhealthy diets and lifestyle
- Infiltration from the unseen energetic world

The constant bombardment of information, especially information that is out of your control, can leave us feeling helpless and overwhelmed. We need to remember to focus on what we can control and what we can change.

Heavy energy can manifest in many ways. We need to take a hard look at how we are conducting our lives. Unexplained medical issues are common physical signs of dealing with heavy energy. These energies weigh heavily on the body, and the body's response to them varies from person to person. Depression, anxiety, and brain fog are some of the most common physical symptoms of dealing with heavy energy.

There are many techniques for managing and releasing heavy energy. Get moving! Exercise. When we physically move our bodies, it helps to shift and release heavy energies. Eat clean foods. Many times, when we have heavy energy with us, we may feel like we need to eat carbohydrate-rich foods. Avoid processed foods, too. One of my favorite things is to drink hot water with lemon.

Mark off items on your to-do list. Uncompleted goals or action plans can create fear-based stagnation within us. This can make us feel paralyzed.

When we work on healing and doing the hard spiritual work to heal our souls through various techniques, such as EFT tapping.

Get outside and walk around barefoot in the earth if you can. There has been a lot of research about the concept of earthing, walking barefoot in the grass and earth. The world is a conductor of free electrons, and walking barefoot allows our body, mostly made of water, to absorb the nutrients within the planet. Earthing does not cost money; it also gives us time to meditate as we walk around. This simple exercise is a great way to release heavy energy.

One of the best ways to reduce and remove heavy energies is to learn how to clear yourself and your spaces. In my book, _Soul Tribe: Navigating the Spiritual War_, I detail how to clean and clear you and your spaces.

Intuition is our most vital psychic ability. When we learn how to tune into our intuition, we begin to connect to our Higher Self and the higher realms. As we learn to harness our intuition, we will also find that our levels of wisdom increase, allowing us to take better actions and react better to life's events.

When we learn to transform and transmute heavy energies, we will find that positive change replaces what was once heavy and overwhelming energies. Learning Spiritual Self-Defense strategies and how the unseen energetic world affects us gives a solid foundation for our soul's health and wellness.

CHAPTER 28

· · · ◆ ◆ ◆ · · ·

FIVE TYPES OF HAUNTINGS & HOW THEY CAN AFFECT YOU

When we think of the word "haunting," we tend to think of ghosts. But did you know there are many types of hauntings, and they can affect all of us, regardless of personal belief systems?

A haunting is an unseen, energetic force that can impact us in many ways. These unseen energies are all around us. Sometimes, we may see something out of the corner of our eye. Sometimes, negative thoughts, thoughts that are not our own, can impede our thinking. Sometimes, our past can haunt us with would've, could've, and should've with past experiences can haunt us. Our emotions, such as guilt, shame, and blame, can haunt us.

As with any form of haunting, we must clear those energies so they don't harm us or hold us back.

Five Types of Hauntings and How They Can Affect You:
Understanding how hauntings work and how they affect us offers us insight into other dimensions and how they work, but we also need to proceed with caution and logic.

1. Residual Hauntings: Imprints of the Past

    Our souls are eternal, and when we reincarnate here, we can carry with us those old emotions that can create unexplained blockages that need to be released through intrapersonal work or even a past life regression.

2. Intelligent Hauntings: Conscious Spirits Interactions

    Unfortunately, many in the spiritual communities don't have a basic understanding of Spiritual Law and how the spirit energies work. Many have preprogrammed beliefs about ghosts. One is that they have unfinished business, and that is why they have not crossed over. Or that they died too soon. These concepts are dangerous to the ghost soul. When a person dies, and they do not cross over to the higher realms, it puts their soul in danger of dark entities soul-napping them.

    Beings or entities from the higher realms will not haunt us, as that is a violation of Spiritual Law. They cannot violate our free will. They are allowed to assist us with our permission. Many times, people will assume a dark entity is a light being from the higher realms. It's always important to vet who or what you might be engaging.

3. Poltergeist Hauntings: Distinctive Physical Disturbances

    A poltergeist is a ghost who has the energy to cause physical disturbances, such as moving things around your home or even physically attacking or harming a living person. Most ghosts do not exhibit those types of behaviors, as it takes a lot of energy to do so.

Dark entities are usually the ones responsible for this type of activity. They can be lower realm intelligence, black magicians, or even extraterrestrials, such as greys or reptilians. These beings can shapeshift to pretend they are light beings.

4. Demonic Hauntings: Malevolent Non-Human Entities

These are what I call dark entities. They do not have our greater good in mind. They are here to harm us and harness our energies for their use. There are many types of dark entities, and each species has political hierarchies to them.

5. Interdimensional Hauntings: Phenomena Beyond Our Realm

Any form of haunting that involves a conscious energy from another dimension that impacts our mortal, third-dimensional world is an interdimensional haunting. This is considered paranormal, which means that it cannot be explained by mortal science and involves supernatural forces.

There are many signs and effects of hauntings. Some examples include but are not limited to, unexplained anxieties, unexplained scratches or bite marks, brain fog, harmful thoughts, a sense of being watched, or hearing voices when no one is around.

When someone experiences signs of being haunted, it can be difficult to feel like we are maintaining our sanity. This is because we live in a physical realm where we can see, touch, hear, taste, and smell. When we come to understand that we are spiritual beings having mortal experiences, it can help us make sense of our situation.

We need to take our power back and clean and clear those unseen energies so that they don't impact us. It can be hard work, but it is possible.

When I first started encountering the paranormal, I was a school teacher. One day, the dark forces came crashing through, and I didn't know what to do or how to remove them. Keeping my sanity was tough on a good day.

There were times when I would be home alone, and this being would come up behind me and choke me until I passed out. I would wake up with bruise marks. There were hot and cold spaces in the same room in my house. The ability to sleep became a distant memory.

Do not engage with them—request help from the angelic realms to remove what is haunting you. Learn how to raise your vibrational frequency and how to clear your home. Look for objects in your home that may create openings. If you find anything that might be used as an opening for dark energy, break it and dispose of it.

It's perfectly fine to seek outside help from a spiritual practitioner who knows what they are doing. Anyone you desire to help you, ask them questions. The most important question is how they clear themselves between clients. Also, if your practitioner is in poor health or engages in low-frequency activities, be wary. If you don't feel like you have a good connection with that person, it's ok to say that and seek other help. Your soul is worth the best. Trust your intuition.

Look at how you are living your life. Some certain negative habits and addictions can create weaknesses within us that give the dark side easier access to us. I am not saying that to make anyone afraid, but knowledge is power. Creating regular spiritual practices, such as meditation and prayer, can also help.

If you sense that you are being haunted, it may help to create a journal of the paranormal activities. Look for patterns, such as time of day, what happens, and the like. If you are seeking more knowledge about how the unseen, energetic world works and how to defend yourself, you may find these online courses helpful: https://thekarmicpath.thinkific.com/

CHAPTER 29

···✦✦✦···

WHAT IS ENTITY ATTACHMENT?

*A*n entity attachment is the concept of some force that overshadows or attaches to us, to our soul. Many types of entities exist. Understanding how the unseen world works is critical to keeping your soul healthy and free of dark entities. Most of the work I do is to remove these forces from families and homes. There is a wide variety of these entities. Because of this, I rarely use the word "spirit." For me, it is not specific enough to know what I am dealing with.

We live in the third dimension. This is the land of time, space, and dimension. These elements give us our physicality. The ability to see, touch, taste, hear, and smell. Many nefarious entities reside in the fourth dimension, the hells, limbo, lower astral. These beings fell from the light of GodSource and used human energies and frequencies to feed and sustain themselves. They do this by attaching it to us in a variety of ways.

If we can't see them, then how can they exist? It wasn't that long ago that people didn't believe washing hands could save lives. Until the invention of the microscope, we were not able to see viruses and bacteria. These elements went unseen by the naked eye. The same is true for unseen entities. Sometimes, our technologies can capture unexplained phenomena.

A spirit entity attachment is an unseen entity that gains access to our energy field and utilizes our energies for its benefit. At the same time, they do harm our souls. These attachments can also mitigate our free will by planting thoughts in our heads that are not ours—and getting us to react to situations in a manner that would not be our norm.

Many factors can create an entity attachment. However, the bottom line is that it comes down to the person's frequency, soul history, and soul strength. How do we conduct our lives? Do we compromise ourselves? How do we treat others and ourselves? Are we of service to self or of service to others? When we treat ourselves well and are working towards the betterment of humanity, it makes it more difficult for them to gain access to us.

Living a mortal life is not easy, and many of us experience traumas. These traumas create cracks in our foundations that give these dark entities access to us. It's not fair, but nothing is fair in war, and we are amid a spiritual war with these beings. However, when we learn to heal those traumas, we take our power back and regain our soul sovereignty. If we don't tend to our wounds, these cracks increase in numbers and can grow deeper. We all experience traumas to some degree; the more we seek healing and learn from them, the stronger our soul becomes.

Addictions are a form of trauma and self-inflicted abuse. It's also worth noting that addiction is a spiritual issue. Why? Because addictions are perpetuated by dark entities. They will do everything in their power to keep a person addicted because this gives them easy access to their soul energy. Overcoming an addiction may be one of the hardest aspects a person can do. However, once the entities are removed and the person's field is protected, removing the addictions may become substantially easier.

There are many signs that you may have an entity attachment. There are physical signs such as unexplained scratches or bruising, chronic fatigue, and odd sensations such as buzzing or tingling.

Some mental signs of entity attachment are brain fog and the inability to concentrate, disturbing nightmares or thoughts that are not your own, or hearing voices in your head that do not have your greater good in mind.

There are emotional signs such as unexplained anxiety or fears. Mood swings and excessive crying without a reason may also be indications of entity attachments.

Perhaps you are always feeling like you are being watched, or you see something out of the corner of your eye, such as a dark shadow or a silhouette. These are all psychic awareness signs that there is something that is not quite right.

There are also several environmental signs that you have dark entities around you. Objects may move or disappear. You may find you have chronic mechanical, plumbing, or electrical issues in your home. You may also feel like your home is never clean.

Some Common Types of Entity Attachments:
There are many types of entities out there. These are three of the most basic types. Ultimately, they all have the same agenda- to take our energy and to lower our frequency so that they can have easier access to us and even our loved ones.

The Hitchhiker

These types of beings latch onto us. They create a low-key fatigue. We may sleep all night and still wake up tired. Or we may not be able to sleep at all.

The Parasite

There are many types of parasitic entities. These guys are the low man on the totem pole. They drain us of our energy; then they must forfeit what they got to their bosses, so to speak.

The Possessor

These guys are the ultimate bad news. They can overpower a person's soul and take over the physical body. When I have a client with this type of possession, removing the entities is one step, but soul retrieval is paramount. Then, it is crucial to close all the openings in our energetic field so others can never enter that space.

Can Entity Attachments Be Removed?

Entity attachments can be removed. Depending on what they are, how they got there will determine how to remove them. Some methods are helpful. These are all a form of spiritual practice, and they do take practice.

What does spirit attachment removal entail? When I work with a client, safety is paramount. We will work together as a team in this process. If you are hiring a practitioner to help you, ask them questions. Ask them about their processes. Look at that person's general health. Are they a smoker or an alcoholic? Are they chronically ill? If there are any red or even orange flags, run. Your soul health deserves the best. There are practitioners out there who may not fully know what they are doing or are flat-out charlatans.

If you suspect you have a negative spirit energy attachment, please note that sage does not work. Sage is the dark entity's tool to make us complacent so that they can continue to gain access to our soul energy. Sage is antimicrobial and tasty in some foods. But it does not have the spiritual horsepower to rid one of dark entities. It's a bunch of dried, crispy leaves from a bush. Folks, if sage worked, this planet should not have any dark entities left on it, as this is what most people do in desperation. I know; I have tried it, and it never worked.

One is to visualize a salt rain pouring you're your home and spaces. Salt cleanses in all dimensions. Lower-frequency beings can't handle this and must let go.

Using high-frequency essential oils such as frankincense will also aid in shoring up your energy field.

Connecting to GodSource, the Divine, Higher-Self through prayer and meditation is also helpful. This is not meant to instill fear but to give us knowledge because knowledge is power.

CHAPTER 30

·· · ✦ ✦ ·· ·

WHAT IS A DARK ENTITY & HOW DO YOU GET RID OF THEM?

*T*he question of dark entities and how to rid ourselves of them is gaining more awareness and traction as we consciously embark on our ascension process. There are many dark entities it's a "Who's Who in the Spiritual Zoo." Each species of dark entity carries its own set of politics, hierarchies, and how they attach to us. The "why" is almost always the same: they need our energy to sustain themselves.

Dark entities are glorified parasites. Meaning we don't need them; they need us. When these entities left the light of God, they no longer had an energy source. In their need to refuel themselves, they found humanity and realized that we all come from the light of GodSource energy.

First, we need a basic understanding of dimensions. As humans, we exist in the third dimension. This dimension has time, space, and gravity. We have the time and physical space to have the experiences we need and the gravity to anchor us into this dimension.

When we leave our physical bodies, we are supposed to go from the third to the fourth dimension to raise our frequency before ascending to the higher realms (fifth and above). When the dark entities left GodSource energy, they ended up hijacking the fourth dimension. Not only do they now call this their home, but this is also the same dimension in which ghosts reside. This is the most important concept we need to understand. Ghost energy, former humans, are stuck in this dimension, and ghosts need help to cross over, no matter how they live. It's not up to us to judge where someone goes upon death.

These dark entities also capture soul nap and ghost souls. They can also reincarnate ghost souls and when this happens, the dark side has perpetual access to their souls. There is no soul healing and restoration afforded to them from this lower dimension. They end up being reincarnated more and more broken in many ways. It's heartbreaking at best.

This is also one way in which these dark ones can capture family lines. Have you ever wondered why certain negative family traits get passed down, such as addictions or sexual abuse? It's because the dark entities have access to our souls. It sounds scary, and it is. However, it can also be as simple as one family member choosing to break free, and that has the potential to shift the entire family lineage.

These dark entities don't want us to realize that they exist. They want to remain hidden from us. They want us to reject the idea of their existence as a form of cognitive dissonance.

Why? Because this gives them the upper hand in their pursuit of humanity.

Energetic disturbances can vary widely from constant electronic, plumbing, or mechanical issues. You may feel as if a room or space feels oppressive or uneasy.

If you find yourself suddenly having mood swings, such as crying without any reason, this is a good indication that something in the energetic world is amiss. Unexplained anxieties and suddenly feeling angry or fearful are also good indications that you may be in the presence of dark entities.

The Five Tips for Removing Dark Entities:

1. Cleansing and Purifying Your Space

   The phrase, "Cleanliness is next to Godliness," is an important one to remember. Keeping our physical spaces clean and free from clutter, dust, and the like increases the frequency of our home. When a home space is unorganized, cluttered, and dirty, energy stagnates and does not flow. It invites "lower realm entities" into your home. These are the small, wispy little guys whose job it is to upset us and our loved ones over inconsequential matters. They then give the energy that they extract from the humans to their bosses.

   There are a million recommendations on the internet that tell us how to cleanse our spaces. Frankly, most are less effective. If they were, we would not be having this conversation. Any citrus essential oil can help to shift the energy of a space. You can add it to a spray bottle of water and spray areas that you sense are negative or of a lower vibration

2. Seek Professional Help

   If you feel inundated by dark forces, you may need to seek a professional to help you. If you are seeking outside help, make sure you are going to work with someone with a proven track record, is in good health, and is willing to explain to you what is happening and include you in the process. Never, ever take someone else's word as gold about your situation.

3. Strengthening Your Spiritual Protection

   We have been in a spiritual war for millennia. It's time we took a hard look at our spiritual practices and discerned what was working and what was not.

4. Raising Your Vibrational Frequency

   When it comes to raising our vibrational frequencies, find one to three new elements that you want to try. Incorporate them into your spiritual practice routines and evaluate them in a month or so. How have things changed? Have there been improvements?

5. Inner Healing and Self-Reflection

   Looking at how we conduct our lives, looking for negative patterns, and evaluating how we act and react to situations around us is an essential act of self-reflection. Spend time with yourself. If you find you don't like to be alone with yourself, why is that? After all, you are your soul and are you avoiding something that would be helpful to address?

   Doctors and lawyers have practices, right? Why shouldn't we also have our practices, our spiritual practices? When we create consistent and protective spaces, the benefits are limitless.

This is key to keeping the dark side out. If you are new to these concepts, start small. Start with a three-minute meditation in the morning or evening. Play Mozart or other proven high-frequency music in your home. Don't trust someone else's YouTube rendering of their high-frequency music. How would you know? If you look at Dr. Masuro Emoto's work, Messages from Water, he shows us how the vibrational frequencies of Mozart's music balance and lighten the crystalline structure of water.

These dark entities want us to bury our heads in the sand and not acknowledge that they exist. This gives them the upper hand. Look at them from a logical viewpoint and remove your fears. Fear in small doses, is designed to keep us safe. Fear in large doses is paralyzing and makes us ineffective.

We are in physical bodies, and this is our superpower. These dark ones are in violation of spiritual laws, and with proper guidance, discernment, and education, we can properly and permanently remove them and take our power back.

CHAPTER 31

···◆◆◆···

WHAT ARE ETHERIC IMPLANTS & HOW DO THEY AFFECT US?

*T*o better understand the concept of an etheric implant, we need to understand that we are multidimensional beings. Our souls are eternal. We have lived many lifetimes, and our souls exist between lifetimes. The human soul is not the only type out there in the universe. Some countless other beings and entities exist outside of our earthly time, space, and dimension. I find it interesting when people talk about searching for life on other planets because they are assuming that life on other planets must look like life on our planet. This is a narrow way of thinking.

If you have listened to some of my YouTube videos, you may have heard me speak about the spiritual war we are in and the importance of building a healthy soul. The concept of an etheric implant is that it is an energetic force that influences us in an inorganic manner. These types of implants may be designed to keep us from succeeding in many aspects of our lives. These implants can control us in many ways. They are designed to suppress our frequency, to hold us back.

There are several ways in which etheric implants can come about. One manner is negative emotions such as guilt, blame, and shame. This trio of emotions is often preprogrammed. Beliefs stemming from childhood can create cracks in our soul's foundation. This trio of emotions is low vibrational and can keep us in fear mode. These types of emotions should be considered opportunities for growth and increased self-awareness. When we work hard to overcome obstacles in life by removing negative patterns, we grow spiritually. Spiritual growth is about attaining knowledge and wisdom as we move about on our karmic path.

Emotional implants tend to look, feel, and respond as energy blockages. Clearing up an energy blockage may be relatively easy, but we must also do the hard work of explaining why and how it got there. Suppose you grew up in an environment where you were verbally assaulted and belittled, never having the opportunity to learn to stand up for yourself. In that case, you may find that as a teen or adult, your body rings with fear when speaking your truth. Or it may have caused you to have uncontrollable anger outbursts. These are a form of emotional, etheric implants that you can remove by learning strategies to use your voice and speak your truth. This may not happen overnight because what you are learning to do is to break a detrimental pattern. When you do this, you also help those around you to grow by leading by example.

Entity attachments are one of the main causes of etheric implants. (This is where you may wonder if Laura also writes science fiction.) This is the big and scary one for most folks. But remember, knowledge is power.

There are many types of nefarious entities and beings out there that need our energy. When these beings left the Light of GodSource, they quickly realized they needed an energy source because they no longer had access to the Light. Their 'aha moment' was humanity. They discovered humans are direct GodSource energy and if they can tap into our fields, they can then sustain themselves.

One way they do this is through etheric implants. We need to remember and reinforce the concept that they need us; we do not need them. The way they interfere with us is also a violation of Spiritual Law. These beings are very similar to parasites. Parasites that reside outside of the third dimension.

Mental illness may be a separate issue. If you are struggling mentally and are becoming overpowered by harmful thoughts, you may need to speak to a medical practitioner.

Yes. The Light Side, the benevolent beings, such as angels, cannot manipulate us in this manner, as it is a violation of our free will. Humanity was gifted the concept of free will so that we may learn and grow on many levels. Etheric implants mitigate our free will as these energetic devices are meant to control our behaviors, siphon our energy, and may even cause physical ailments that are unexplained by the medical communities.

Etheric implants are designed to act as controllers, dumbing us down, making us complacent, and keeping us sleeping. Often, these implants will influence our emotions and behaviors so that the dark entities can harvest these energies. But we do not have to comply. Again, knowledge is power.

Etheric implants tap into our energy fields, usually through our chakras, but not always. There are many types of implants, and each type has a specific purpose and action. When I work with a client, I will remotely view their energy field with them, looking for implants to remove them and find the cause. This is sophisticated, energetic work.

One common example of an etheric implant is these devices that look like battery watches and have these fine filaments, or threads. At the other end of these filaments is another small implant or device. The issue with these is that one must be extremely thorough in the process. Many times, they are attached to the heart. The heart is considered to be the seed atom of the soul. This gives them direct access to your soul.

Some of the physical signs you may be dealing with an entity implant are you may be chronically tired, and have odd body sensations such as buzzing, humming, tingling, or numbness. One of the more common elements is a nonproductive cough. This is a chronic, low-key cough that seems to last forever. There appears to be no reason for it. You were never ill. Or if you were, it was months ago, and this cough still lingers.

Others may have more mental signs that something is amiss, such as thoughts that are not your own, such as, "Why am I thinking this?" You might hear voices in your head that don't have your greater good in mind. You may have difficulty concentrating and experience something called brain fog.

There are also emotional signs that may lead one to consider they are dealing with etheric implants such as mood swings, unexplained anxieties or fears, and sudden emotional outbursts such as crying without reason. For those more sensitive, you may feel that something seems off without much explanation.

We can learn how to remove etheric implants. The key is frequency. Learning how to raise our frequency is a constant process. At the most basic, bringing elements of joy into your life, going outside in nature, and playing high-frequency music are some ways to raise the frequency of you and your home. The more we work on improving our frequency, the harder it is for these dark ones to attach to us.

Retain your soul sovereignty. "I do not consent to any implants or negative entities to be in my space. I hereby request all implants to be removed. RIGHT NOW." This mantra is helpful, but please note there may also be other elements that need to be addressed before this can fully work.

Etheric implants that are emotionally driven energy blockers can be removed as you continue working on improving your spiritual path. Etheric implant removals are considered safe; however, it is always up to you to find a reliable practitioner. This is always your responsibility because you are your soul. Such removals may help you as you move forward in life.

During an etheric implant removal, some people may feel sensations of slight tugging, pulling, or a release. You may also feel significantly lighter and see more clearly. You may feel unexplainably brighter, as it is a sign of soul health and wellness.

What Should I Do If I Think I Have an Etheric Implant? I encourage anyone who may suspect they have some of the signs listed above to consider looking for a well-qualified practitioner to help. Ask them what their experiences are, what are the expected results, and how the practitioner clears themselves between clients. Your soul's health and well-being are worth it!

CHAPTER 32

···◆◆◆···

WHAT DOES A DARK ENTITY MEAN IN DREAMS & WHY ARE THEY THERE?

*D*ark entities in dreams are nothing new and they can be and represent a vast array of elements. These dark thoughts can represent anything from conflict in our lives that we are trying to work out in our sleep state to coming across negative entities as we astral travel or even having full-on psychic attacks. Sounds scary, but knowledge is power.

Dark entities, also known as demons, exist in the unseen world, the 4th dimension. These beings left the light of God and when they did that left also left their energy source, their food supply, so to speak. When they did that, they had to get creative to find an energy source to sustain themselves- and they found humanity.

We are all multidimensional beings, and while we live a mortal life, we connect to other dimensions and entities. When we sleep, we often leave our physical bodies and travel astral. We could be meeting up with our deceased loved ones, working with our spiritual teams, or getting harassed by dark entities.

Dark entities in dreams are where nightmares, night terrors, and sleep paralysis can stem from when we sleep. Many times, they affect children more than adults. It's also quite common for medical professionals to say that night terrors are a normal part of childhood. Since when should terror be a normal part of anything we experience?

Even in ancient Mesopotamia, the Roman Empire recorded the concept of demons inhabiting our sleep. Cultures and locations throughout the history of our planet all have some sort of texts or stories that discuss these entities and how they affect us in our sleep.

Psychological Interpretations of Dark Entities Masquerading as Family Members in Dreams

We need to remember that not every negative element we experience is a negative paranormal issue.

I remember years ago, one of my children would wake up in sheer terror in the middle of the night. There was a pink monster that would come at her and terrorize her. This was happening over and over, and I started to wonder if something was going on in her kindergarten class as she started to not want to go to school. I started asking questions about her day, and it turned out that a neighbor boy, who was also in her classroom, was tormenting her. Once we shed light on that and spoke with the parents, the nightmares ended.

If you or your child are experiencing recurring nightmares, it is worth looking into aspects of your life that might be negatively affecting you.

Dark entities in our dreams can represent a myriad of issues. Sometimes, it can help us solve a problem or force us to work through a situation we are dealing with in our daily lives. However, it may also be possible that you have unwanted visitors that are not psychological.

When we don't work on our inner fears and anxieties, when we don't deal with our problems, they can seep into our dream state. We need to be able to work through dark and negative emotions and feelings so that we can get to the other side. If we allow the fears to grow out of control, fear becomes paralyzing and limits us. This ultimately lowers our baseline frequencies.

You may find that keeping a journal next to your bed. This way, when you wake up, you can immediately write down your thoughts and dreams. Start to look for patterns.

Ask for angels to come in to protect you and your family. Angels are one of our most underutilized resources and all we need to do is ask for their help. One of the most important things we can do is to keep our room clean and free of clutter. When we go to sleep in a clean and organized environment, it calms the mind.

Turn off your electronics, phones, computers, and tablets for two to three hours before you go to bed. Studies have shown that blue light emitted from electronics may alter our circadian rhythm and suppress the secretion of melatonin, negatively impacting our ability to get a good night's sleep. (https://www.health.harvard.edu/staying-healthy/blue-light-has-a-dark-side)

Use essential oils, such as lavender, chamomile, or frankincense, in a diffuser as you go to sleep. This can help to shift and calm your brain chemistry and raise your vibrational frequency.

If you are experiencing repeated nightmares or are physically being harmed while you sleep, request that angels from the higher realms fill your room and home and give them specific instructions. There may be times when professional help may be in order. This is especially true if you feel that you are experiencing negative entities that are robbing you of proper sleep.

CHAPTER 33

·· · ♦ ♦ ♦ ·· ·

CAN DARK ENTITIES APPROACH ME WHILE LUCID DREAMING?

*D*reams have been a fascinating aspect of humanity for as long as humans have been sleeping. People have equated dreams with premonitions and spiritual experiences, but what if a dream is more than that? I am sharing a true story of a lucid dream I had.

Is lucid dreaming different than other dreams? When we think of traditional dreams, we tend to be retrospective. If we remember our dreams, they tend to have current life problem-solving thoughts in them. Lucid dreaming happens when the person is aware they are dreaming when you know that it may be more than a dream.

The following is a true story of a lucid dream with a physical manifestation.

I saw myself leaving my body. I can't explain it, but I know I didn't want to go. It was as if there was some external force taking me. This force felt dark and heavy. I wasn't able to see this force. I didn't know what it was. I couldn't scream for help. I couldn't move my body. It was frozen.

The only aspect I knew I had was my mind, but everything was moving so fast. I was confused. Then everything went black. I was floating. I had no idea where I was and still couldn't move. Then I "landed."'

I was transported to this large stone building. It felt like we were all in a church-type setting, but not. The room was large and cold. The walls were about 20 feet tall and made of grey stone. The side walls were dimly lit. Just enough to see shadows. There were about 50-75 others there, as well. We were all standing in rows. I was in the center row of the group and to the right side of the building. It was as if there used to be pews or rows of seats. Now, there were dividers between the rows, about waist high, also made of grey stone.

I didn't know anyone, and we weren't allowed to see faces. We were told to look down until told otherwise. The voice was somewhat electronic sounding. We were all wearing dark brown robes with capes. Then I realized in front of us was an altar, with a table in the center. At the altar, six hooded figures were on each side of the table, and one taller hooded figure was behind the table, for a total of 13. I immediately knew that the tall one in the center was the one that transported me there.

The altar was about half the width of the room. It seemed very Medieval. There were wrought iron gates on the sides. They could have been doors. I wasn't sure. That's when we were all handed crystal wands. The feeling of this crystal wand was beyond terrifying, and I didn't know why. It was heavier than normal and about 20 inches long. It looked black, but also everything was dark.

And that is when I realized what was about to happen. I saw this white goat standing in front of the table at the altar. We were given instructions on using these wands to mutilate these goats and this instruction period seemed to last forever. It was about the control of the crystal wand. How to use crystals for black magic and ultimate power.

The fear and panic inside me were overwhelming. I could not do what they were telling us we had to do. We were told failure would equate with our personal torture. A goat would be replaced with anyone who failed or refused to do as told.

I slowly started to look around. That is when I realized behind us was a set of very large and heavy doors. One was not fully closed. I had to figure out how to swim upstream how to move in the opposite direction of the crowd without being noticed. I could hear the goats moaning in torture and these sheeple passing their tests. To this day, this makes me sick to my stomach.

I really focused on trying to become invisible as I slowly made my way backward and toward that door. Touching the door was terrifying. I thought for sure I would be detected. As I touched the door, I slipped through.

I immediately woke up and sat up in my bed. I couldn't catch my breath. It felt like my heart was pounding outside of my chest. I was breathing hard. Then I thought to myself, "Wow. What a dream. Where did that come from?" All while still feeling terrified.

An important side note: Three months prior, I had purchased this six to seven-inch smokey quartz crystal wand.

It had clear points on each end and was rather symmetrical. I remember when I bought it, questioning the purchase because smokey quartz really wasn't my thing. When I got home, I placed this crystal wand on my nightstand and kind of forgot about it.

I looked at my nightstand and suddenly realized this was no dream. That smokey quartz wand took a hit for me. It protected me. The back half of it disappeared. The bedroom was carpeted, with no hard surfaces. I tore my room apart, looking for shards of crystal, the missing part, never to be found.

I keep this crystal with me to remind me of the work I do and how dangerous it can be. It also reminds me of how important this work is. I keep it with me always.

Can you change the outcome of a lucid dream? Throughout this event, I kept reminding myself that I was in control of my mind. Our minds are our most powerful asset. We need to remember that. When it comes to lucid dreams, if we are aware enough, we can change the outcome.

Set intentions before going to sleep. Setting intentions, praying for protection, and utilizing your spiritual tools before sleep can help offset any negativity. I realize I went through that experience for a variety of reasons. One is that I learned a lot. The second is that, as I grew in spiritual strength and stamina, I learned how to remove those entities and, in the process, free those animals, along with many humans.

We can use lucid dreaming to work with our spirit guides, to set intentions for greater knowledge, and so much more.

CHAPTER 34

...•◆•...

WHAT ARE REPTILIAN SHAPESHIFTERS & ARE THEY REAL?

Reptilian shapeshifters were outed in the summer of 2023 when a woman on an airplane saw one. The reality of this situation created a form of cognitive dissonance for many people, calling her crazy or mentally unstable. So, what really happened? My thoughts on this are that there was another passenger who was inhabited by one of these entities, and it decided to have some fun with this woman and reveal itself to her for a moment. Reptilian shapeshifters left the light of GodSource, and they need our energies to fuel themselves. It's that simple and that sick and twisted. These entities wreak havoc on so many of us every day.

Can reptilian shapeshifters be natural, or are they a science fiction phenomenon? Science fiction is always based on some sort of reality. Think about the expression that art imitates life. Why is this? For example, in the Harry Potter series, the Dementors are a real type of dark entity that swirls around us. The author somehow was gifted that knowledge, and it was put into this series to show us who and what they are but disguised under the concept of science fiction.

The first question we need to address is what a shapeshifter is. A shapeshifter is someone or some entity or being that is not portraying themselves as they truly are. An excellent example of a shapeshifter that we can all relate to is the all-too-familiar story about a beloved priest who ends up being a child pedophile. We expect him to be one thing when, the truth is, he is a monster.

There are several species of reptilians. The larger ones tend to be more of the physical warrior types. The smaller ones are the ones who are the overseers and give directions. Many times, they have red or yellow eyes. The ones with the yellow eyes have pupils that are vertical, and not round. You may see a fleeting image of yellow eyes or some shadow out of the corner of your eyes.

Reptilians are one of many alien entities that are influencing so many of us. In a nutshell, the reptilians are the ones who created the Communistic form of government we see on our planet. They utilize humans as worker bees. They will infiltrate governments and inhabit our global leaders. If you are sensitive enough to see between the dimensions, look at some of our global leaders, and you may see some physical anomalies. They can come and go into humans. As they do this, they take over that human's soul. In essence, they kidnap the soul. We often think of the concept of a kidnapping as purely third-dimensional. This is why creating a healthy and strong soul is vital to our soul sovereignty. They cannot access us when our soul is strong. As a side note, the Greys are responsible for our capitalistic societies of debits and credits. ☺

Pretty much all cultures have words or concepts for these entities. The Chinese have dragons. The Maya have Chaac; the Aztecs have Tlalac. There are Jinn in the Middle East. The Christians have the serpent in Genesis. All cultures throughout history have words and concepts about reptilians.

Future proves past. What I mean by this is that throughout ancient lore and myths, we have heard about these entities. Now, with the advancement of technologies, our cameras and videos capture elements that were once thought of as myths, such as ghosts and portals. I have a trail camera that I use just for this purpose. It's a part of my defense system. There have been images of entities trying to break through. In one series of photos over the course of an hour, you can see the entities breaking through and my spiritual team removing them.

I love a good skeptic because they help me to create a logical trail behind what is happening in the unseen, energetic world. Sometimes, there is information that can be so debilitating that people form a sense of cognitive dissonance. There are people in certain religions who absolutely hate what I do. They consider my work to be "of the devil." They can't bear the thought of this reality, and this is their form of protection.

Shapeshifters are entities who can read our minds and portray themselves as our inner desires or even our greatest fears. Creating a strong mind and soul means they have a tough time accessing you.

Are Reptilian Shapeshifters Dangerous? More than likely, yes. However, it is said that there are a few here who have been able to elevate their consciousness levels and are now working to help the benevolent galactic federation and humanity.

Break any contracts you may have with them. You may have heard of people making statements such as, "I do not consent." Each one of us has many types of soul contracts. When it comes to contracts and nefarious entities, many times, these contracts are not true to you. These are either false contracts, contracts of omission, or contracts where we are forced into something because of them mitigating our free will. We have a right to break these contracts. When we do this, we regain our soul sovereignty.

Learn to raise your frequency and keep working on your spiritual practices. Learn to use discernment when communicating or contacting any type of being. Never, ever assume you are speaking with or working with a specific entity without testing them.

CHAPTER 35

···✦✦✦···

WHAT ARE THE GREYS & WHY ARE THEY SO COMMON?

*W*hen we think about aliens, most of us picture Greys, those thin beings with spindly limbs, large almond-shaped heads, and black eyes. These are the extraterrestrials we think of when it comes to alien abductions, which drives our curiosities and fears. Since the 1940's it appears there has been an uptick in their sightings. However, there have been recorded sightings throughout our history on this planet.

Trigger Warning: This information has come through a variety of sources, including interactions with clients. We need to remember that when we work on creating a healthy soul, it denies access to harmful beings.

Many times, people will contact me because they have missing time or odd health issues that are never properly diagnosed. I did regression with a client to find out why she had missing time and health issues, leading us to the Greys in a most unusual way.

Greys and other extraterrestrials are usually interdimensional beings, meaning they can transcend time and space. They use specialized technology to phase in and out of physical bodies while on the Earth plane. When it came to the famous Roswell crash, was that ship's technology destroyed? Leaving EBE1 (Extraterrestrial Biological Entity) in a physical form and unable to shift back into an interdimensional state?

There are many theories about who they are and from where they originate. It is said they come from the binary star system Zeta Reticulae. It is thought that they are here to experiment on humanity.

Encounters with Greys are not for the betterment of humanity. They have a hive-mind mentality and are interconnected through their technologies. I was hired to remove a large cluster of greys that had invaded a series of office spaces. They were constantly being spotted by the surveillance cameras. What was interesting is that on these cameras, you could see these small white balls floating in the air and landing on a person. Then, within hours, that person was in an altercation with someone else. That floating ball would then disappear through the wall, which was their main portal. This group of greys was experimenting on the people in that office space.

With the onset of technology, our cameras can more easily detect the presence of orbs, ghosts, and extraterrestrials. This helps us to remain in control and keep our power.

There are many abductees/experiencers who have reported seeing different types of grey aliens. There are several species of greys, tall whites, and zetas, which are larger and usually the overseers and brokers between them and other species, such as reptilians, mantids, and others.

Biological Grey Drones have been created in laboratories and are not able to maintain a natural biological/spiritual connection, nor are they able to evolve on a spiritual level. This is problematic as they see no reason why their abductions of people are a big deal. They have lost their moral compass, and coupled with military grey technologies; they have no problem experimenting with us.

Their bodies are generally weak, but they do have superior mental and telepathic abilities. They can control humans and animals they are abducting with their psionic abilities.

They can clone and replicate their consciousness. I worked on a project a few years ago where Greys were experimenting on groups of children and adults who they deemed to have higher levels of consciousness. They wanted to know why and how to stop this group's evolution, as they found them threatening to their mission. This group of tall white greys was found all over the security cameras. In fact, you could see them planting devices on the people to modify their behaviors. I called these devices "scouts." These little balls of light were shown to land on people and then within an hour that person would be in an irrational conflict with another person. This was all caught on security cameras.

The Greys don't care about humanity. They are more scientific in nature and abduct us and run all sorts of experiments on us.

Roswell Barney and Betty Hill were a couple who, in recent times, claimed to have been abducted in 1961. Their case drew national and international attention and popularized the greys, adding to lore and legend. What I find interesting is that their memories failed to be wiped after the abduction. They had clear recall of the spaceship they were on and what happened to them. This was the case that created an emergence of Greys within American pop culture.

What Do Greys Want? Testing and harvesting our DNA. They have evolved out of the ability to procreate and thus need human DNA and human hosts.

Biological Grey Drones have been created in laboratories and are not able to maintain a natural biological/spiritual connection, nor are they able to evolve on a spiritual level. This is problematic as they see no reason why their abductions of people are a big deal. They have lost their moral compass and, coupled with military grey technologies, they have no problem experimenting on us.

Their bodies are generally weak, but they do have superior mental and telepathic abilities. They can control humans and animals they are abducting with their psionic abilities.

They can clone and replicate their consciousness. I worked on another project where Greys was experimenting on groups of children and adults who they deemed to have higher levels of consciousness. The Greys were threatened by this group and wanted to know why and how to stop this group's evolution. They felt this group could alter their mission. This group of tall white greys was found all over the security cameras. In fact, you could see them planting devices on the people to modify their behaviors. These "scouts," or little worm-like entities were shown to land on people and then within an hour that person would be in an irrational conflict with another person. This was all caught on security cameras.

The Greys don't care about humanity. They are more scientific in nature and abduct us and run all sorts of experiments on us.

Greys heavily impact our human existence, especially in the Western world. They are responsible for our economic system, the concept of credits and debits. Greys have replication technologies and as they accrue credits, they can replicate their consciousness to multiple locations.

Greys are also those extra-terrestrials that are known for alien abductions. When they abduct a person, they often experiment on them, they can place trackers and other devices within us, and will harvest our DNA. These seem to be the three main stories that abductees will report.

Greys will also create false contracts with humans they have abducted. In most cases, these contracts are not above board. The contracts they try to create with us are contracts of omission, leaving out pertinent data, and false contracts based on lies. They do this to gain control over us and mitigate our free will. It is up to us to realize and break free from these falsehoods.

To gain control over humanity, they have begun to implement The Transhumanism Movement- the pursuit of the capture of the human soul. There seem to be more and more people whose thoughts are so ingrained they are not able to change or adapt any belief system; they become irrational at certain elements in the news, and they cannot seem to think for themselves. Another clue can be people whose eyes are black or vacant, and they lack any form of a moral compass. This can be an indication that a person's soul is in jeopardy.

Greys may be one of the most popular extra-terrestrials; this could be because they resemble the human figure, and there is slightly less form of cognitive dissonance when it comes to seeing a Grey versus an Insectoid.

Greys are telepathic and can use their minds to do their work. Many abductees report that they are frozen, unable to move or speak, but that the greys are communicating with them. This adds an element of fear if not full-on terror. Some are thrill seekers and actively seek out encounters. My advice is to be careful.

Greys have had a large impact on science fiction. Why is that? Because, in many cases, science fiction isn't so much fiction. Our writers and entertainers get their information from somewhere. For example, J.K. Rowling's dementor beings, those dark, shadowy, wispy creatures that fly around, are reported by people all the time.

Greys have become a part of many conspiracy theories, from government disinformation campaigns to mind control experiments to helping to create the New World Order.

If you feel you have been abducted, have unresolved conflicts, or struggle with soul sovereignty, it may be worth working with a qualified spiritual practitioner to see how you are being influenced and then to break those chains to retain your soul sovereignty.

Part Four

·····◆◆◆·····

LIGHT BEINGS

CHAPTER 36

···✦✦✦···

WHAT IS SPIRITUAL DISCERNMENT?

Spiritual Discernment is the ability to distinguish between safety, harm, or negative thoughts by using our senses- to make out, to reason, to recognize, to tell apart. When we are dealing with the spiritual realms, we are looking between dimensions. This is especially important when we are working with our spiritual teams and our spirit guides.

We need to understand that we are spiritual beings and there are many dimensions or realms with which we connect. Not all the beings and entities are who they say they are. It's no different than in our physical world. A beloved priest turns out to be a pedophile, for example. That priest is not who he says he is. The same exists in other dimensions. The ability to learn to discern who or what we are communicating with is critical for our soul health.

What happens when we think we are talking or working with Arch Angel Michael? Is he a shapeshifter or impostor being? This is more common than we may like to admit. This is the crux of the situation. We need to understand that the dark side relies upon our naiveness or laziness.

The ability to avoid being deceived is difficult in our third-dimensional world. How do we trust? How do we know that something is for our greater good or not? We need to apply these concepts to the spiritual realms as well.

Is discernment a spiritual gift? Discernment is not a gift. It is an ability that is learned and earned. Spiritual discernment is key to our soul health. The more we learn to discern, the stronger and healthier our soul becomes. Spiritual discernment is the most important work we can incorporate into our spiritual growth.

We need to start by learning to develop and trust our intuition, our most valuable psychic ability. It's our intuition that keeps us safe and connects us to our spiritual teams. It's our intuition that helps us to grow spiritually.

There are many ways to practice spiritual discernment. Many ways are through visualization techniques. Our mind is our most powerful asset. We can do much with the power of thought. Have you ever heard the concept that thoughts are things? Our thoughts can be quite powerful.

In my book, _Soul Tribe: Navigating the Spiritual War,_ I discuss many aspects and elements of spiritual discernment. Let's say you are trying to meditate and connect with your spiritual team. It's important to validate to whom or what we are speaking or connecting with. One of the easiest ways is to visualize yourself pouring salt on any entity you are communicating. Salt cleanses in all dimensions. Please close your eyes and sense where your guides are that you are trying to connect with, and visualize yourself pouring salt on them.

If they disappear or shapeshift, it means you dodged a bullet. If they remain the same, it means you have the guides from the higher realms. You can also use frankincense oil or any other high-frequency substance.

In the spiritual realms, we need to understand that there are many types of beings and intelligences that may not be for our greater good. If they can gain access to us through trickery or deceit, they will. They will create a crack in our foundation, which will erode our soul's health.

Learn to trust yourself. Many of us have had our intuition beaten out of us as children; we were told to stop imagining and stop believing. This is also an opportunity for us to learn how to regain our intuition. There are practices and exercises that you can do to improve your intuition. It can be as simple as writing three words on three pieces of paper and feeling the energy of the words to select if you have the correct one. This takes practice.

How do you know if you are excelling in spiritual discernment? How are you living your life? What are you doing to resolve any problems or issues? Does life flow smoothly for you? Are you finding you are on an accelerated path for learning? These are some of the signs that what you are doing is working for you. It's also important to mention that even those of us may seem to be on a more difficult path. Sometimes it is what we choose. We may choose to learn how to overcome financial difficulties or learn how to leave an abusive situation. The point is we are learning and evolving. It's not always pretty or easy, and we need to understand that this is why we are here and what we are here to learn.

All of us will go through a variety of challenges. It's how we learn to act, react, and grow from them that enables us to evolve, or even de evolve on a spiritual basis. The ability to enhance our discernment skills allows us to develop our intuition and grow spiritually.

Learning spiritual discernment and spiritual self-defense strategies will help us cultivate a healthy soul and create stronger connections to GodSource and our true spiritual being.

CHAPTER 37

···◆◆◆···

THE FOUR TYPES OF SPIRITUAL ENERGY & HOW THEY AFFECT US

*T*here are many types of spiritual energy. It's important to understand that energy comes in many frequencies, and not all frequencies are optimal for every person. Just because it's considered spiritual doesn't mean it will be good for you. I'll explain.

We are multidimensional, energetic beings. Everything we do and everything that surrounds us carries a frequency or a vibration. Spirituality is all-encompassing. We are all spiritual beings interacting with one another and having spiritual experiences.

Energy knows no boundaries and is in continual flow. Energy can also become blocked and stagnant. Learning how to clear energy blockages and to improve the flow of energy will help enhance our vital life force.

The Four Types of Spiritual Energy & Their Unique Characteristics:

The unseen, energetic world impacts all of us. There are four basic concepts of spiritual energies. Each of these energies carry with them specific characteristics.

1. The Vital Force: Pranic Energy

    Prana is life force energy; it can also be called chi or qi. That which gives us life sustains us. It permeates and is within all living beings. This life force energy is within us all. We can enhance our pranic energy in many ways, from breathwork to consuming healthy foods. Practicing yoga is also said to help with the flow of prana.

2. The Emotional Current: Emotional Energy

    Emotions are pure energy. Each emotion carries with it a frequency or a vibration. Stephen Hawking's Power vs. Force book shares his map of consciousness, which measures the frequencies of our emotions or consciousness. For example, the emotion of shame has a vibrational analysis of 20, while joy is at 540.

    When we talk about our emotional state, it's important to be authentic with our understanding of our emotions. Pretending to be constantly happy to raise your vibration is spiritual bypassing. We need to do the work to achieve happiness or any other vibrational state we desire.

3. The Power of the Mind: Mental Energy

    Our minds are our most powerful asset. When we learn how to harness the energy and the power of the mind, we dramatically shift our vibrational frequency and embrace life experiences with a sense of heightened wisdom.

4. The Universal Connection: Spiritual Energy

   Spiritual energy can also be thought of as soul energy. The mind, body, spirit, and consciousness are the all-encompassing soul energy that we all exist within.

There are many ways we can enhance our spiritual energy. The goal is to create a solid baseline energy. This way, when life knocks us down, we tend not to fall as hard and are able to rebound and recover faster. Practicing gratitude will do a lot to enhance our spiritual energy and help us with our ascension process.

Learning how to heal our hurts and wounds will also help. It's important to understand that healing has no earthly timeline. The ability to heal old wounds and traumas happens in degrees and layers.

Prana comes from the Hindu philosophy, and yoga is one way we can learn breathwork. There are many benefits of breathwork, such as the ability to achieve deeper sleep, help to balance blood pressure, reduce depression, and help with mental clarity.

Our emotions are a powerful energy force, and when we learn how to harness that energy, we can manipulate and control those detrimental emotions to transmute them. The ability to control our emotions can be especially helpful when we are dealing with negative emotions to ensure we don't contaminate others. For example, if you find yourself extremely angry, those emotions can, and often do, contaminate the energy around other people. Energy has no boundaries.

Our minds are our most powerful asset. Our minds process emotions, helps us to make decisions, and can also connect us to higher sources for answers. Learning to be mindful and present helps strengthen our intuition.

Learning to improve our intuition, connecting to our Higher-Self, and learning to connect and grow our spiritual teams will all deepen our spiritual connections. One element to consider is learning how to discern who or what we are communicating with when connecting to our spiritual teams.

When karma is out of balance, there is tension. When we experience tension, this is a huge sign that we are out of balance. The ability to figure out what is out of balance and why is key to ensuring we are spiritually healthy.

When we feel stuck, when we are unmotivated, and when we experience unexplained anxieties or fears, that is a sign that our subconscious is trying to tell us that there is a blockage. There are many ways to clear energy blockages, and the first is to identify if something is amiss. When we are dealing with energy blockages, sometimes mediation and prayer can help. If that doesn't work, you may need to find a trustworthy spiritual practitioner to help remove those blockages.

When our energies are in harmony and alignment, the sky is the limit. This means that we are actively working on healing and ascension.

As we learn to work with energies, how they impact us and how they affect us- both positively and negatively- is all a part of learning who we are and how we are here to serve humanity. When we connect on deeper levels, we are better able to connect GodSource energies and improve our soul health.

When we learn how negative energy forces can impact us, we will learn how to protect ourselves against the negative, energetic world. This includes low vibrational frequencies, dark entities, and so much more. Knowledge is power. The more we know, the more we know.

CHAPTER 38

···✦✦✦···

WHAT IS YOUR HIGHER-SELF? (HOW TO CONNECT TO YOUR HIGHER-SELF)

*T*here is a lot of talk about the Higher-Self in spiritual communities. It's a common buzzword. And for those unsure of what the Higher-Self is, it's kind of hard to ask because of the heftier egos that reside within many spiritual communities may make us feel deflated or ignorant on such an important topic. First, you are your soul. Our soul encompasses our Higher-Self. It is an aspect of who we are, and we are multidimensional beings that are extraordinarily dynamic.

In a nutshell, our Higher-Self is the wise, light, and love-driven aspect of ourselves that can guide and assist us while we are living this mortal life. The Higher-Self is also the rational and logical aspect of us that can give us guidance without being clouded by our emotions or knee-jerk reactions to difficult situations.

Some characteristics of our Higher-Self include a sense of calm and compassion. Our Higher-Self knows and understands we are living a mortal life for the experiences our soul needs. Our Higher-Self also has a sense of kindness and patience with us. It doesn't overreact to our decisions and our Higher-Self is there to help keep us on track as best as possible. Our Higher-Self is in harmony with us and the Universe.

There are many benefits to connecting with your Higher-Self, such as the ability to overcome negative self-talk and negative patterns in life. When we can focus and connect with our Higher-Self we find clarity, balance, and abundance as we move forward in our mortal lives. One of the most important aspects is that connecting to our Higher-Self, it helps us to lead our life with wisdom and discernment, which allows us to grow on our spiritual path. When we are well connected to our Higher-Self, we will feel less anxiety and less harmful thoughts, and it will connect us directly to GodSource energy.

We need to learn to pay attention. It's that simple. But in our modern times, we are constantly inundated with all sorts of distractions and our time seems more limited than ever. I urge everyone to take some quiet time for themselves to get centered and aligned. It can be hard to carve out those pockets of time, but remember, even five minutes is helpful.

When we connect with our Higher-Self, we are open to receiving Divine guidance that puts our soul into alignment with the universe. We may be better able to see and sense the world around us with a pearl of enhanced wisdom, make better choices, and find our relationships smoother.

The ability to connect to your Higher-Self is a spiritual practice, meaning we need to practice and learn. The ability to connect with our Higher-Self on a deeper level requires us to learn to trust and develop intuition. Our intuition is our most profound psychic ability. Contrary to popular belief, it's not seeing dead people. When we focus on our intuition, it means we are directly connecting to Higher-Self. Our intuition is what keeps us safe on many levels.

Many of us have had to relearn how to develop our intuition from childhood. This is part of the spiritual challenges many of us face, how to enhance our intuitive abilities.

It's crucial to know that when we connect to our Higher-Self, we never need tools of divination, such as cards. The reason is this is a form of spiritual bypassing that often creates avenues for dark entities to pose or superimpose over your Higher-Self and lead you in a less-than-desirable direction. Know that you have the power within you and trust yourself in this process. It's essential that you own your soul and you do not hand off your power to any form of divination tool.

The ability to slow down our thoughts allows us to listen to that inner voice, the one that carries with it the wisdom that guides us. Many times, the thought of doing a meditation seems overwhelming. We have heard about people who spend hours on end sitting in a lotus position on top of a mountain in deep meditation. The reality is that all we need are a few moments of quiet and solitude. Maybe it's in your car on a lunch break. Or maybe, upon waking in the morning, instead of hustling out of bed to start the day, give yourself the gift of 10 minutes to focus and be mindful of being in those moments. Plan out how you want your day to go. It doesn't have to take long. Mindfulness is simply allowing yourself to be in the moment. These are both spiritual practices, meaning we get to practice over and over. After all, there is no learning in perfection.

Any form of journaling, whether it is contemplative, asking questions, or seeking information, is helpful as it is a form of self-reflection. This helps us to create a stronger connection to our Higher-Self. Date your journaling experiences so that you can go back and reread what you have written, and chances are you will be pleasantly surprised with the information you have been writing.

Take some time and look back at your life, what went well and what were some of your struggles? What did you learn in those moments. This is what our Higher-Self desires for us- soul growth.

There are many types of intuitive practices that we can employ to help us develop our intuition. Look at these practices as a type of game. Get three note cards and write one word on each one. Mix them up and start to work on feeling the energy of the words on those cards and pick up the card with the word you are thinking about. This is also a form of energy work as you are feeling the energy elicited by those words.

Another practice is to lie down and spend time sensing your body. Wiggle your toes and work your way up your body. This puts you in tune with your body, which houses your soul, deepening your connections. When we strengthen our connections to the Higher Self, we strengthen our connections to the Divine, to GodSource energies.

Connecting with your higher self is a powerful form of self-care. The ability to communicate with our higher self is the most powerful form of self-care. This unites our soul, making it more robust, and your soul is worth investing in your higher self.

CHAPTER 39

···◆◆◆···

WHAT IS LIGHT LANGUAGE & HOW CAN IT BE USED?

*T*he concept of light language has been gaining in popularity. But what is it exactly? Is it some type of woo-woo, sage-wafting, airy fairy lingo? Or is it real?

Light language transcends the human condition, meaning it is a language that bypasses our written and spoken words. There are no physical actions, symbols, or hieroglyphs associated with light language. This language is a vibration that speaks directly to our spiritual DNA, our soul essence, and other light beings. It communicates with the soul. It can, however, be facilitated through the human body.

Light language is multi-dimensional, transcending time and space. It's a high-energy source of frequencies, vibrations, and information that come through sounds, tones, body movements, or written symbols or scripts.

It is said that light languages hail from other planetary systems, mostly Starseeds, such as Arcturian, Pleiadian, Sirian, and Lyran.

Some say that the origin of light language is a form of communication that lives within our souls. As we ascend, it may become more innate and pronounced within us. It is also said that it is the language of the stars and is very much soul-healing.

Light language comes in many forms. Not one form is more correct or powerful than another. It's about what works for you.

Light language can appear in many forms, sometimes it is spoken or sung and there are no words to it. It is simply vibration. My friend, Abby Lynn is an amazing practitioner and I have the privilege to be in a ceremony where she uses light language to clear and heal people and places. This is a quote from her: "People often ask after they have heard light language for the first time, 'What was that and why did my body react the way it did and why am I emotional?' My answer is simple, you have just heard a language that only the soul knows, you were remembering. Light language is energy and frequency, a language that is simple yet so complex it ripples through the quantum field. Light language is something that is meant to be felt, not heard, and it will enter and move throughout your auric field exactly where it is supposed to; it is a language for the soul." https://abbylynn.co/

Light language can also come from auto writing, but the writing is more in the frequency of the signs and symbols that come through you. The 'writing' medium can be anything from standard pen and paper to sand to paint. The medium is irrelevant. It's about what comes through you.

Many times, people can feel light language pour through them through authentic binaural beats. Binaural beats are a phenomenon that occurs when listening to two frequencies at one time. Hence, the term bi, meaning two. When these beats are sustained for certain periods of time, it alters the brain waves to promote relaxation and healing.

I used the term 'authentic binaural beats' because there is a lot of choices out there and it is imperative for your soul's health and well-being that what you are listening to is for your greater good. How do you know it is, and why? ALWAYS ask those questions. If you get a low-frequency set of binaural beats, it can open you up to dark elements.

Light language is all about frequencies, and its general purpose is to help us to increase our frequencies. One thought about light languages is that they are multidimensional healing frequencies. They can also bring in new information to us that will become activated within us when we are ready for it. This can also be an aspect of a spiritual awakening.

The purpose of light language is to raise our frequencies and promote ascension as we heal old traumas and wounds. These traumas and wounds can transcend lifetimes and be carried within our DNA. Light language has the capability to release and heal ancient emotional and physical wounds.

If you are looking for a light language practitioner, I highly recommend Abby Lynn. She is a serious practitioner who studies constantly. Her website is abbylynn.co.

Light language can do a lot for us as we continue our spiritual paths. Light language becomes more readily accessible to us as we continue with our spiritual practices, such as meditation and prayers, and enhance our spiritual toolboxes. Remember to give yourself the gift of time. Time to explore, learn, and appreciate who you are and how far you have come. Spirituality is not a contest, and we are exactly where we are supposed to be.

CHAPTER 40

•••••◆••••

WHAT IS A LIGHTWORKER
& WHAT DO THEY DO?

*T*he term lightworker is a relatively new one, but the concept of a lightworker is not. In fact, the word lightworker is not even in the dictionary. A lightworker is on a spiritual path who seeks the greater good. The 'greater good' can mean many things to many people. A lightworker is about being of service to others.

There are two types of service: service to self and service to others. When we are of service to others, that naturally lends itself to being a lightworker.

A lightworker is a person who has a calling within their soul to do spiritual work for humanity, GodSource. They also seek greater spiritual knowledge to make a difference to humanity and our planet. It's purported that many lightworkers come from Starseed origins, but this doesn't have to be the case. Their goal is generally to raise the vibration and awakening of the planet and its inhabitants.

A lightworker is always a person who is in progress. In other words, a true lightworker is always evolving. They never stop learning; they are always evolving.

Ideally, lightworkers are here to heal, help others to heal, and to bring light and hope to our planet. Let's face it, our planet is not an easy place to be. Mortal life here can be hard and full of traumas, dramas, and other obstacles. A lightworker can take those obstacles to learn from and grow.

Being there for one another and learning how to heal, in all aspects is critical for soul advancement on our spiritual paths. Learning how to work with our emotions is also important because when we let our emotions override us, it creates cracks in our foundation. When that happens, the dark side can enter within us.

A true light worker knows that we are to never stop learning. Our ability to learn may ebb and flow, as the knowledge and energy imparted upon us may need to settle in as we learn what to do with that. With that, a true lightworker is here to share their knowledge with others. We need to learn to work together and not be in competition with one another.

The ability to learn how to channel GodSource energy and transmute that energy to facilitate healing is powerful and carries with it a lot of karma. Ensuring that you are tapping into the light and not being fooled or tricked by dark entities is paramount for you and anyone you work with for your soul health.

There are many types of lightworkers. I always hear from well-meaning people that they want to know what they can do spiritually to help the planet and humanity. This answer is true for everyone: find your passion. Take your passion, learn, grow, and that will unfold into being of service.

Types of Lightworkers and Their Unique Roles:

1. The Empaths: Emotional Healers

   Many lightworkers are also empaths. Empaths find that they are sensitive to all types of external energies. It could be the Wi-Fi around them or a busy shopping center full of chaotic energy. It could be an angry co-worker or a grieving family member. A lightworker must learn how to know when emotions or feelings are not their own. They must also learn how not to absorb those energies which are not theirs. When we take on other people's 'junk' we can cause harm to ourselves and need to learn that we are not martyrs in these cases.

   Detached compassion, the ability to understand how someone else is feeling and not take on their emotions, is a sign of strength, maturity, and someone with an increased sense of wisdom about themselves. It doesn't mean we are emotionless robots, but when we allow ourselves to be overwhelmed by other people's dramas, it makes truly helping them rather difficult.

2. The Messengers: Communicators of the Divine

   There are lightworkers who carry light codes within them and communicate with true light beings. We all have spiritual teams who guide us. Our spiritual teams are in flux, as they are here to help us with what we need. They are also karmically earned. Whenever a lightworker communicates, it is their responsibility to know if they are truly from the light side. We all need to examine whomever a light worker is communicating with, knowing that there are shapeshifters and nefarious forces out there who love it when we "just assume."

3. The Transmuters: Neutralizing Negative Energy

    Everything is energy. We all have the ability to manipulate energy, but that comes with great responsibility. When we can transmute negative energy to a neutral or a positive force, that is of great service. One way to transmute and shift energy is by learning to use a violet flame.

How can you recognize a light worker and their traits? Some people incarnate knowing their soul's purpose; for many, it will reveal itself when the time is right. We are all different, and that is the beauty of humanity. Many lightworkers feel as if they have a higher calling, they are passionate about helping others, and they may have gone through a process known as the Dark Night of the Soul.

Be aware of the false lightworkers.

A true lightworker is here to help. A false lightworker may show their true colors by appearing to be all-knowing, wanting to control others and other people's knowledge. They can be quick to dismiss you if you have a differing opinion. They are often covert narcissists hiding behind the guise of spirituality.

On a personal note, one of the more profound learning experiences in my life was from a false lightworker. I learned a lot from this person, and it took me time to detangle myself from this person. This is where the dark side got greedy because this person unwittingly made me stronger and more knowledgeable to help others. I am grateful to this person. It was a lesson that I needed to learn. I share this because true lightworkers learn from one another.

How do I know if I am a lightworker? Ask yourself: Are you a kind person? Do you care about the well-being of others? Do you seek to learn more about GodSource? Do you seek greater spiritual knowingness? If the answer is yes to any or all these questions, you are a lightworker.

Lightworkers are human, and we are not here to live perfect lives. Learn to embrace what you are learning and be grateful for your experiences. Our experiences make us who we are.

CHAPTER 41

·· • ✦ • ✦ • ··

WHAT IS A STARGATE
& ARE THEY REAL?

W hat is a stargate? A stargate is an energy wave system, or vortex, that can connect multiple dimensions within the universal time/space matrix. It's an otherworldly portal to other dimensions. This means that, in theory, as they can connect to multiple dimensions, it offers extraterrestrial beings access to our planet.

The concept of stargates became more widely known and discussed through the fictional series, Stargate, which is based on an alien wormhole device that enable teleportation throughout the cosmos.

As there is more awareness around spiritual aspects of ascension, more information about frequency and vibration, coupled with the onslaught of modern technologies, there has been a marked increase in interest and study of stargates.

Ancient buildings stand the test of time and go beyond ancient technologies all over the planet. For example, there are pyramids all over the planet. Many times, when we say pyramids, we think of ancient Egypt. There are also many pyramids all over Mexico and other parts of the world. Their constructions are still a mystery.

This is just food for thought. When Jesus was on this planet, he was 'missing' for 18 years. What if he traveled to other parts of the world? It is said that Quetzalcoatl appeared before the Mayans at that time. Some circles believe that he was in India as well. If this is true, how did he do that? Did he use Stargate technologies to become a time traveler?

Have you ever noticed that ancient civilizations never left any documents or data behind? Who were these ancient beings, and what was their role on earth?

The Incas believed that their civilization started when light beings entered the mountains through a portal. Could this have been a stargate?

The ancient Greeks talked of portals that they could use. They even described one that was thought to be a portal to hell. The Muscogee people in the southeastern United States have created the serpent mounds, where extra-terrestrials are said to have come and gone.

NASA has admitted to spending time and resources over the past couple of decades trying to uncover the myths and mysteries of Stargates. Jack Scudder, a plasma physicist who worked for NASA, has discovered a unique way to discover indications of portals through technology and using the earth's magnetic grids. While this is a simplified explanation, you can learn more about plasma and its applications to discovering space and astrophysics. https://www.colorado.edu/physics/research/plasma-physics

Also, The U.S. Army established the Stargate Project in 1977. The goal was to look for and find psychic phenomena, like stargates, and look for potential military applications. Since then, there have been many "spin-off" military projects.

It is purported that there are 12 stargates on this planet. Some people say there are only two. However, if we think of a stargate as a portal or a wormhole, there could be countless numbers of them.

Sri Lanka's Stargate Mystery: In the center of three famous temples in Sri Lanka is an ancient chart that is said to be a map containing codes that unlock the Stargate. To date, it remains a mystery.

Stargates are an intriguing overlap between reality and science fiction. This concept tells us that our minds are powerful, creative, and insightful. Over the past several decades, there has been a huge uptick in Stargate storylines. One must ask why. Is it just sci-fi fantasy? Or are there hints of realities within the storylines?

Ancient Aliens, Skinwalker Ranch, Star Trek, and many other movies and books have storylines and plots enmeshed with stargate concepts. Is truth stranger than fiction?

This is where we can agree or agree to disagree, right? Regarding the paranormal and concepts like Stargates, you need to decide what rings true for you and ask yourself why or why not.

As Hiromu Arakawa stated, "There's no such thing as no such thing." Meaning that there are many other worlds and dimensions outside of our planet Earth. Is it possible that they are also all interconnected through stargates? And lastly, if NASA and the US Army have investigated the stargates, one would think there might be something to it.

CHAPTER 42

··· ◆ ◆ ◆ ··

WHAT IS A GUARDIAN ANGEL?

*T*he guardian angel, our protector who watches over us as we journey through life, is an elusive mystery. How do you know you have one or more? What do they look or feel like? Stay tuned to discover seven signs your guardian angel is trying to contact you. Guardian angels are often considered essential to our spiritual teams, our Soul's Tribe.

Where Do Guardian Angels Come From? The angelic realms come from higher dimensions and do not experience time and space as we do. They were created to assist humanity as we live our lives on this planet. They must abide by spiritual laws and cannot interfere with our free will. This means they cannot tell us what to do, say, or how to act or react. But they can and do love us immensely.

We need to understand some basic tenets of Spiritual Law. GodSource gifted humanity with free will. We are afforded free will to help us to grow on our spiritual paths. We are gifted the ability to make choices without interference so we can learn and apply lessons. Angels are here to assist us, but they cannot interfere with our free will. This means we must ask them for help and guidance.

Does Everyone Have a Guardian Angel? Not everyone has a guardian angel. Our spiritual teams are karmically earned. Also, it's important to note not all spiritual teams and guardian angels work for the light side. As shocking as this may seem, if there is anything you take away from this article, this little nugget bears repeating: *Not all spiritual teams and guardian angels work for the light side.*

We have heard of the concept of fallen angels, those light beings that left the side of God in the Lucifer Rebellion. The dark side will try to trick us into accepting a false guardian angel. However, we do have the upper hand because we have free will. We need to learn how to vet or weed out the dark ones.

Here are tools you can use to vet your guardian angel and other members of your Soul's Tribe—work on keeping your frequency elevated as much as possible. When working on contact with your guardian angel or any other being on your spiritual team, visualize yourself pouring salt all over them. Salt cleanses in all dimensions, and these lower-frequency beings cannot handle the frequency of salt. You can also visualize other substances, such as frankincense oil.

If what you are hearing or sensing from them does not sound right, chances are you have an impostor being. Call upon the higher realms to remove it *right now*. When you do this, you may feel an immediate energy shift.

How Do I Know If I Have a Guardian Angel? This is a great question, and the answer comes down to how you are living your life. Are you kind, compassionate, and in service to others? Then, chances are pretty good that you have a guardian angel.

Those who are in service self, narcissistic in nature, harm animals, and this type of personality may not have a guardian angel. However, it is important to mention that when a person begins to change their ways for the betterment of their soul and learn to help others, they can earn their guardian angels.

Seven Signs Your Guardian Angel Is Trying to Contact You:

When attempting to connect to your Guardian Angels, it's critical to always vet them. You oversee your soul and who you choose to come into contact with. Please don't assume it's the good guys. Many other impostor beings will try to infiltrate your team. They do this in an attempt to gain access to your energy field. Remember, we do not need these dark entities. They need us. They need our GodSource energy to sustain themselves. This is not much different than how parasites find their hosts.

1. They Come to You in Your Dreams

   Dreams may be the most common way our guardian angels contact us. This is because when we are sleeping, we tend to astral travel. During this time, we may have meetings with our Guardian angels. Upon waking up, write down your immediate thoughts about your dream state. You may start to find patterns.

2. Sudden Temperature Changes

Sometimes, we may sense a cooling and loving sensation in the air around us. Sometimes, it can feel like a warm hug.

3. Unexplained Physical or Emotional Sensations

When I first started noticing my angels, I could feel them. They felt like bubbles on my left arm. I didn't know exactly what that was, but I started seeing and talking to them regularly as I started paying attention. Another common sensation is a tingling sensation at the crown of the head.

4. You Hear Voices or Unexplained Sounds

Clairaudience is a form of psychic hearing. Angels are interdimensional species. Hearing angel voices may sound melodic or even musical. Many times, we need to almost guess what they are trying to tell us. It can be like that child's game telephone. Eventually, you will be able to understand what they are trying to communicate with more ease.

5. You Begin to Notice Signs & Symbols

Common angelic signs are repetition of numbers or other patterns, cloud formations, or dreams. Other signs in nature, such as hawks, may represent them and let you know you are protected.

6. You Notice Repeated Occurrences of Angel Numbers

These number patterns or sequences are one of the more common ways they use to communicate with us. The number 1111 may mean you are on the right course. The number 333 represents positive energy and starts your plan of action.

7. The Sudden Appearance of Feathers

Angels' wings often look like feathers to the human eye. This substance is called vril, a form of their energy. If you are finding feathers, look for the metaphor. What is your angel trying to communicate with you?

Learning to pay attention to signs from your guardian angel is a spiritual practice. The universe wants us to know that we are connected to our guardian angel and that we are loved. There is no one right way to communicate with your guardian angel. Meditation, prayer, walking in nature, and being mindful and present in the moment are all ways we can learn to build our connections to our guardian angel.

CHAPTER 43

···✦ ✦ ✦···

SIX TYPES OF SPIRITUAL GUIDES & HOW TO COMMUNICATE WITH THEM

*T*here are many types of spiritual guides, and learning to discern who they are, where they come from, and how to communicate with them is vital to your soul's health and wellness.

Understanding Spirit Guides and Their Impact on Our Lives

When we are born, we all have a spiritual team. These entities are ideally here to assist us on our mortal journey. Our spiritual teams ebb and flow, come and go, depending on our deeds and actions.

It's imperative to understand that we all have spirit guides, our Soul Tribe. What we need to know is that not all spirit guides pitch for the same team, meaning our spirit guides are karmically earned. Learning to call upon our guides with intention and discernment helps us create, build, and maintain a healthy soul.

The most significant element to understand is to learn to assess if the spirit guides you communicate with are yours *and* for your greater good. We often assume who or what we are communicating with is who they say they are. The dark side depends upon our complacency.

For example, if you believe you are working with Archangel Michael, how can you vet that process to ensure you don't have an impostor? In our physical, third-dimensional world, we would never hire a babysitter who is a stranger to take care of your baby. We look for recommendations, check references, and do background checks to make sure that person is safe to leave your child.

Why should you assume that your spirit guide is a good guy without a vetting process?

There are many types of spirit guides. They come from many parts of the Heavens or higher dimensions. How can it be that Archangel Rafael can help so many or be called upon by so many at the same time? Because he isn't encumbered with a physical body. He is an energetic signature, allowing him to be in multiple places and situations simultaneously. Below are just a few examples of spirit guides. Every organization has a hierarchy. The angelic and all other dimensions are no different.

Six Types of Spirit Guides:

1. Archangels

   These guys are the big deal. They have a very large, energetic signature about them and, often, a specialty. For example, archangel Rafael can be called upon for healing elements for which you need assistance.

2. Guardian Angels

   Many people in the spiritual communities will say we all have guardian angels. This is not always the case. What type of guardian angel do you think Jeffery Epstein had? Get my point?

   They are karmically earned. It's also important to know that our guardian angels cannot interfere unless we ask for their help. Don't be shy when asking for their help. The more we ask, the deeper our connections become.

3. Spirit Animals

   I work with a young woman in the UK who has a white wolf as her spirit animal protector. She mainly interacts with him in her sleep state. He is there to guide and protect her and has warded off negative entities for her. They are a team, so to speak. An impostor wolf would come in a couple of times, but she knew something was off.

4. Ascended Masters

   These light beings have a highly evolved level of consciousness that has gone beyond the reincarnation cycles. They have chosen to grace the earth in human form for humanity's development and evolution. Jesus, Mary, and Buddha are examples of ascended masters.

5. Departed Loved Ones

   There is a common misconception that when a child dies, that child automatically becomes an angel. When our loved ones die, the ONLY way in which they can assist us is when they cross over into the Higher Realms, the

Heavens. If a loved one dies and lingers as a ghost, that ghost energy has a low frequency and will inadvertently cause all sorts of problems, financial and mental health issues, and mechanical issues around the home, such as electrical or plumbing problems.

In the book Soul Tribe: Navigating the Spiritual War, there are strategies you can use to learn how to help your loved one cross over. No one deserves to linger as a ghost.

6. Elemental Beings

These are second-dimensional beings, the Devers, or those who reside in the Devic Kingdom. They are also known as faeries, sprites, and the like. They can only utilize the energies humans give off. When we see angry weather, hurricanes, tornadoes, floods, and fires, this is because nature is out of balance. (Weaponized weather patterns are not included in this.)

Our spirit guides communicate in many ways. We need to learn to pay attention. Look for signs and synchronicities. When you look at the time on the phone, do you see number patterns?

They can send us dreams, advise us when we are sleeping on how to handle situations or help us navigate future events.

They can give us many signs to show that they are with us and that we are not alone. This can be especially helpful when we are going through difficult times. For example, you may hear a song repeatedly coming on.

A synchronicity means that we are experiencing a meaningful coincidence. Perhaps you constantly think of a friend or a loved one, and then they call out of the blue. Your spiritual teams may have helped orchestrate that connection somewhere behind the scenes.

Just like any relationship worth having, we need to put time and effort into it. Give yourself the gift of spending time to meditate and learning how to connect with your spirit guides also learn how to vet them to make sure they are the real deal.

Learning to quiet our minds, to be present and in tune, helps us to learn how to feel or sense that they are around us.

Journaling a conversation with your spirit guides can help you connect with them. If you are trying to figure out how to communicate through writing, start by asking a question and simply start to auto-write what the answers are. Try not to think as you write and simply let it come through the writing.

Learning to vet and assess your spirit guides is the most critical element in your soul health.

Part Five

...•◆•...

TOOLS FOR
YOUR SPIRITUAL
TOOLBELT

CHAPTER 44

···◆·◆·◆·◆·◆···

WHAT IS SPIRITUAL INTUITION, AND HOW CAN IT HELP YOU?

What is spiritual intuition? All intuition is spiritually based. Everything we do is spiritual because we are spiritual beings. However, our intuition is also our most profound psychic ability. Contrary to popular belief, it's not seeing dead people. Our spiritual intuition is designed to keep us connected to GodSource and our Higher Self while living on this planet. The more we learn to listen and trust our intuition, the safer and wiser we become, and the better we shape and direct our lives.

Spiritual intuition is that guiding force, the still, quiet voice that assists and helps us to navigate through life. When we learn to use our intuition, we learn how to respond to elements that affect us. This is an important concept because we all have free will, which means that we make choices throughout our lives based on our experiences. Do you find that you are dating the same personality type repeatedly? Why is this? Is your Higher-Self bringing these personality types into your life so you can learn to trust your intuition and say no somewhere along the way?

What is the difference between instinct and intuition? When we hear the word instinct, what often comes to mind is the word survival. What are the instinctual elements we need to survive? Instincts can be hard-wired within us, such as a fear of snakes or heights. It could be that your spiritual DNA left an imprint from a past life. It could be based on some type of trauma. It could also be a form of self-preservation. It can be a knee-jerk reaction to a situation.

Intuition is a feeling or sense of knowing based on your gut feeling. You are in tune with your body and how your body responds to a question or situation. When you meet a new person, what is your sense of them? How do you feel around them? Is this a person that you would feel comfortable around? The answers to these questions can be based, in large part, on our spiritual intuition.

How does spiritual intuition work? Developing our spiritual intuition is always a work in progress. The more we become GodSource-centered, the more we actively work on connecting with our Higher Self, and the deeper our spiritual intuition grows. The inverse is also true. If we make poor choices or disconnect from GodSource and our Higher Self, our frequency becomes lower, and our spiritual intuition will in to diminish.

e way we can learn to develop our spiritual intuition tate or become centered in our thoughts and ask question about a situation we are grappling with. When we ask a question, we activate our logical, conscious mind. However, the goal is to work beyond our conscious mind of rationalizing and reasoning and start to notice our emotions and body sensations. When we do this, we will start to receive messages that feel like a strong yes, no, or a pull in a certain direction. Many people will call this a gut instinct or an inner knowingness. When we do this, we immediately go past our "Dr. Spock" mind and connect to our Higher-Self.

Spiritual intuition is the gateway to higher consciousness. It is the ability to understand or have that inner knowingness without conscious reasoning. When this happens, we begin to operate on higher levels and have a more profound sense of awareness within.

We are experiencing a global awakening, and our intuition plays a huge role in our spiritual awakening. A highly developed intuition will allow us to learn to grow into our authentic selves as we become more aligned and empowered with our spiritual growth.

The main benefit of developing spiritual intuition is creating a healthier and stronger soul. Our souls are the most precious and coveted aspect of us.

There are also many other benefits to having a healthy spiritual intuition. When our intuition is strong, we learn to listen to the health of our bodies. When does something feel off, and how can it be repaired? Intuition also enhances our creativity, which helps us to make better decisions. Overall, a healthy intuition will help improve our spiritual, emotional, mental, physical, and even financial health. Isn't your soul worth it?

Take a moment, consciously breathe, and learn to feel your body. Ground yourself. If you are surrounded by electronics all day, spend time in nature, take off your shoes, and feel the earth.

When we make the time—and it doesn't have to be a long time—to listen to our Higher Self, it helps us raise our frequency, make better choices, and run our lives smoother. We all face adversity from time to time. We are here to learn lessons and gain wisdom on our karmic paths.

We are our soul. When we learn to embrace and cultivate our spiritual wisdom, not only does it help us connect to GodSource, improve our decision-making, and facilitate our creative aspects, but it also has the power and the potential to affect those around us as well positively. Those around us will feel the positive energy and it may shift their day and outcomes for the positive, too.

CHAPTER 45

· · · ✦ ✦ ✦ ✦ · · ·

FIVE TIPS FOR RAISING YOUR VIBRATIONAL FREQUENCY

*T*he concepts of vibration and frequency have turned into spiritual buzzwords. Everything has a vibration or frequency to it. From rocks and trees to sound and light to cells and molecules, to humans and animals, planet Earth has a vibration or a frequency to it. Even our emotions have a vibration to it. Vibrations are a type of energetic rhythm and flow, the speed at which something vibrates. The real question is, what does this mean for you? Our vibrational frequency is a direct correlation to our levels of consciousness.

Your frequency is your basic state of being, how you feel, how you act, and how you respond to outside stimuli. Think about our homes, for example. Clean homes have sunshine coming through and no clutter or piles. The energy, or frequency, of that home emits a sense of peace, order, and calm. Dirty homes, shades, and blinds constantly closed and full of clutter tend to have occupants that feel chaotic, frazzled, and disorganized. These types of homes tend to have repair needs. This same concept can be applied to our physical bodies and our soul energy.

We may have been born into a family where there was excess chaos and drama, but we all can learn from our parents and those around us to learn how to do things differently. When we learn to raise our vibrational frequency, it helps us to live life with less drama and more wisdom.

Learning the tools and strategies to raise our frequency helps us in many ways. First, we need to understand that our intentions play a large part in the ability to increase our frequency.

The idea is that if we can learn tips and strategies to create a strong baseline when we get hit with something, we don't fall as hard. This means that if we have developed a naturally high frequency and we get news of a death, job loss, or any difficult issue, we can bounce back and recover quicker. We can also act and react more appropriately. A high vibrational frequency helps us grow our wisdom, discernment, and coping strategies.

When we can create a higher vibrational field, it can help keep illnesses away, as a strong vibrational field can act as a shield; think of your favorite superhero.

What frequency do humans vibrate at? The short answer is it depends on the human. J We need first to understand that we are not created equal. We are created in karma, based upon our soul's experiences and the lessons and wisdom our souls are seeking in this lifetime. We all have experiences thrown at us that are unanticipated. For instance, you wake up, get ready for work, and feel wonderful. You drive to work feeling good, and then suddenly, a car swerves into your lane, almost striking you. Your emotions would change from loving and wonderful to possibly angry or fearful. Identifying emotional situations can lead us to understand more about how frequency works.

We need to understand that our vibrational frequencies change constantly. Learning how to raise your baseline frequency can be helpful.

"Just raise your frequency," they say. This is a frustrating answer to those who are trying to understand these concepts. We all have a first day; no matter where you are on your spiritual path, honor that.

There are many ways in which we can do this. One is to look around your home and ask yourself, "Does this (object or room) make me feel happy or fill me with anxiety?" If your answer is the latter, what can you do about it?

Surrounding yourself with music that fills your heart and activities that bring you joy raises your vibrational frequency.

Five Tips for Raising Your Vibrational Frequency:

1. Meditation

   Mediation is listening to God or your Higher-Self. Take a few moments out of your day to sit with yourself and ask questions you are seeking answers to, then listen and feel for those answers. The answers may not come right away, but they will come. Give yourself the gift of patience.

2. Be Grateful & Practice Humility

Gratitude is everything. We need to remember that we incarnate here for the experiences our souls need on our karmic path. There are those who have dealt with extreme traumas and others whose life seems to be a bed of thornless roses. Appreciate who you are, where you come from, and where you are going. At the end of each day, find 3-5 things that you are grateful for. This spiritual practice is extremely powerful. When we can tune into our gratitude, we begin to grow on many spiritual levels.

3. Practice Forgiveness

First, forgiveness is not forget-ness. Forgiveness does not have a timetable. When we are hurt or wronged, know that the ability to forgive may take time, and give yourself permission to be kind to yourself. IF you have done something and are seeking forgiveness, the ability to examine what happened and come up with a plan for healing atonement not only balances out the karma, but also allows for lessons learned and the ability to move forward.

4. Be Good to Your Mind & Body

Learn to spend time alone with yourself. It's an opportunity to reflect upon your personal situations and seek a higher source of guidance.

Examine your emotions. Take the time to analyze your feelings. Our emotions carry an energetic vibration. Emotions such as guilt, blame, and shame need to be released as best as possible. David Hawkins' book Power Vs. Force is a great work on emotions and the vibrational relationships within them.

5. Limit Low-Vibrational Relationships

Look around you and examine your personal and work relationships. How does a coworker make you feel? Is your boss kind and understanding or does he or she make you feel unworthy?

Families are the most blessed unions, or they can cause the most strife in our lives. We all have that embarrassing uncle who drinks too much on holidays or the grandma who nitpicks. We also have very loving and attentive relatives and that is who we would benefit to gravitate towards. Recognizing how these people make us feel is the first step in understanding vibrational relationships.

CHAPTER 46

···✦✦✦···

HOW TO USE THE POWER OF INTENTION FOR PERSONAL GROWTH

*O*ur minds are our most powerful asset, including creating the power of intention. Intention is the starting point when it comes to manifestation. Learning more about the power of intention will help us with manifestation as they go hand in hand.

When we can understand the role of the Law of Intention, we can be more specific in setting intentions. When we focus on setting intentions, we will grow stronger. We need to be exact and understand our intentions' impact on others. For example, if you want a promotion and a pay raise at work, you will set the intention of your new role and its benefits. You will also remove all negative self-talk, as that will cause blockages.

We need to understand that everything is energy. Thoughts are energy, which we can turn into action when we set an intention. The intention is energy, and there are many degrees of intention or the energy we put into a goal or a plan. When we have an intention, we are setting the energy in motion. Also, we need to be flexible with outcomes and timelines regarding intentions.

The Universe requires that we are specific. What are you seeking? What are your goals? In general, not planning is planning to fail.

Prayer without action is simply wishing and hoping. When we pray, we speak to GodSource. When we meditate, we listen to GodSource. In both cases, we can't simply wish for something and have it come our way. While we have the intention, we also need the plan to execute it.

When we set the intention of a new job and raise, take the time to create a physical action plan around that new job. Create a vision board or an outline of the new responsibilities. Make sure to write down your new salary and set the intention of that goal. And don't be shy about it.

It's about the attention of the intention. Be flexible in the outcomes of your intention. If you end up not getting that promotion or pay raise and someone else does, someone else may probably have needed that experience more than you. It's also possible that there is something better coming your way.

Look at what may be blocking you. Is there a pattern that needs to be broken or overcome? Your obstacle may be a part of a karmic cycle that you must learn to overcome. This could also be an opportunity to learn how to reprogram your subconscious mind. If you find yourself making excuses as to why you are unsuccessful or have doubts, you can use the power of intention.

The role of karma in our intentions. As you learn to use the power of intention, it's imperative to understand how your actions and reactions to life events affect others. The power of intention is not meant to take away from others. As you set your intentions, it's essential to understand the collective greater good.

There are many ways to set intentions, including visualization techniques. Learn to see yourself on the other side of your intention's success. How does that feel to you? What does it look like? How do your loved ones benefit?

You are creating a consistent affirmation. Let's say you set the intention to be less shy at work. First, figure out why you feel shy. Is it because you feel intimidated by someone, not as smart, fearful of using your voice? Once you figure out why you feel shy, create an affirmation to overcome that. "I am smart. I am good at my job." Or whatever that affirmation is for you. This will help you to start to reprogram your subconscious mind so that you can break through that barrier.

There are several breathing techniques you can use to help create your intention. When we concentrate on our breathing patterns as we think about our intentions, it helps us to really focus on the intentions. There are many breathing techniques out there, and it's up to you to find what works or doesn't work for you.

When we can learn to measure the impact of our intentions, it helps us to change our behaviors to achieve our intentions. Most of the time, it is something within our behaviors that creates the blockages.

Spend time with yourself. As you do this, you can connect to your higher self. Our Higher Self is there to guide and assist us. You are your soul. As you live your life, we all have the free will to set the intentions to live a life that is fulfilling. Learn to be kind to yourself. Learn to love yourself. As you do this, it becomes easier to feel worthy of your intentions and desires.

CHAPTER 47

···✦✦✦✦···

EIGHT SPIRITUAL GROUNDING TECHNIQUES THAT ENCOURAGE RENEWAL

L earning spiritual grounding techniques allows us to renew, regenerate, and heal the soul. Spiritual grounding is an ancient concept that transcends time. Nowadays, spiritual grounding is more important than ever as our lives are increasingly busy and fragmented.

Spiritual grounding is the ability to incorporate and blend both the spiritual and physical energies of the body and ground them into an earthly experience. When you are spiritually grounded, it means that you can be mindful and in the present moment. This offers us a sense of clarity and centeredness.

We spend most of our days indoors working with electronics and computers. We need to remember to incorporate joy and gratitude into our daily lives. Learning to become grounded helps us feel present in our bodies by eliciting a sense of calm and focus, enabling us to live life more fully and with wisdom.

When we are spiritually grounded, we keep our frequencies elevated, and negative energies impact us less. This allows us to attain inner peace, joy, and creativity, be of spiritual service to others, and problem-solve with greater ease.

There are many grounding techniques that you can find and utilize. The following is a list of eight spiritual grounding techniques you can incorporate into your life as you embark on your spiritual path.

Eight Spiritual Grounding Techniques That Encourage Renewal:

1. Embracing Nature: A Path to Earthly Connection

   One concept that has been around for as long as humans is the concept of "earthing." This is as simple as walking barefoot on the sand, soil, or grass or even placing your hands within the earth.

   When we are one with nature, we can connect to our Higher Self. We can also be alone and learn more about who we are as spiritual beings.

2. Mindful Meditation: A Journey Inward

   Meditation is a gift to our soul. When we allow ourselves the time to meditate, we can start to listen at a deeper, more fulfilling level. Ask yourself what you are seeking. Then, listen for the answers, knowing that they will show up in subtle ways. This allows you to start to tune into who you are spiritually.

3. Crystal Healing: Earth's Gifts for Balance

Crystals offer us many gifts. There are a myriad of crystals available, each with specific purposes. For example, elite Shungite or black tourmaline are good choices if you are looking for added protection. If you are seeking clearer communications, lapis lazuli may be helpful.

If there is an area within yourself that needs to be strengthened or enhanced, start researching which types of crystals may be helpful to you. There are many resources out there to help you find what is right for you. If you find yourself at a crystal store, take your time and try to feel or listen to them. The right ones will come to you.

4. Breathwork: The Power of Controlled Breathing

There are many forms of breath work out there that can help to calm the nerves, get us to focus, and even release stuck emotions within us.

The 4-7-8 breathing technique is one of the more common ones. You inhale for four seconds, hold your breath for seven seconds, and release the breath for eight seconds. The following article is great for learning more about breathwork: https://www.everydayhealth.com/alternative-health/living-with/ways-practice-breath-focused-meditation/

It's important to note that if you suffer from high blood pressure or cardiovascular disease, consult your doctor before implementing a breathwork program.

5. Movement: Physical Activity as a Grounding Force

Moving the body allows energy to flow within us, reducing stagnation and rejuvenating us. It's that simple. Do what works for you. Going for walks, running, yoga, stretching, weightlifting, or any other type of movement helps to reduce so many ailments, from brain fog to stiffness and so much more. Right now, I go kickboxing four to five days a week. It gets me out of the house, around great people, and I get to punch and kick things- for me, this is a win, win, win.

6. Visualization: Crafting Your Spiritual Sanctuary

Learning to visualize to create your spiritual sanctuary allows us to get outside our minds. It can also help us to connect to our Soul Tribe and Higher-Self. Where do you like to go? Is it the mountains, meadow, beach? Start there. If mountains feel like home for you, visualize yourself in the mountains, create a cabin, a stream. This is a visualization technique that will help you to start to learn how to see and feel your spiritual team.

7. Daily Rituals Incorporating Spiritual Grounding Techniques

Daily rituals are practices that we incorporate into our everyday lives, from taking showers and meal prep to meditation and prayer. When we have a routine, it helps to ground us and helps us with our next steps.

8. Journaling: Writing as a Tool for Emotional Stability

Journaling gets things off our chest. It makes our problems less intense. Many times, our fears get in the way of our successes. Fear in small doses keeps us safe. Fear in large doses is paralyzing. Your journal can be many things to you. It can help you manifest your wishes and desires, and it can also remove what you fear by writing it out. Many people have a fear of money, or what happens if they lose their job. Write down the worst-case scenario and ask yourself what is the likelihood that these will happen. Probably not very likely.

Personalize your spiritual grounding practice. Your spiritual grounding practices are just that: yours and yours alone. You do this for you, not your spouse, not your kids, parents, or friends. This is about you. When you give yourself the gift of time, it affords you to be of better and higher quality spiritual service to those around you. It is literally that simple. Maybe one day, you can only do one of your spiritual practices, but the next day or week, you find that you can do many. Let's face it: our days are full, and for most of us, no two days are alike. We are constantly pivoting.

Eight techniques are mentioned above, and you can incorporate any or all of them. It's essential to be realistic in your goals. For example, if you don't live near nature, try to incorporate #6, Visualizing your spiritual sanctuary. Maybe you add some breathwork before your visualizations to help clear your mind. Find what works for you, allow yourself to be flexible with your routines, and most importantly, be kind to yourself in the process. Isn't your soul worth it?

CHAPTER 48

·····◆·◆·◆·····

THE POWER OF PSYCHIC
PROTECTION: GUARDING YOUR AURA

W hen it comes to psychic protection, the strength and
fortitude of our aura is paramount. An aura is an energetic light body that surrounds our physical body and pro-
vides a form of psychic protection. It is designed to help keep
us strong and ward off illnesses and other unseen energies and
entities that may try to steal our energy or harm us. We also
need to understand that energy has no natural boundaries.

One of the best ways to protect ourselves from psychic
attacks is to strengthen our aura or auric field. Raising our frequency is critical. The more we raise our frequency, the stronger our baseline is. This is important to understand because
as we go about life, we encounter all sorts of outside influences that can bring us down, from divorces and deaths to job
losses and health issues.

A psychic attack is best described as being bombarded by lower-frequency energies and entities. Negative energy can leave you feeling irritable, short-tempered, unexplained anxieties or fears, or even a sense that something is off or not right. These are just a few ways we can identify if we are surrounded by or experiencing negative energies.

When this happens, there are a few strategies you can use to help yourself. One is the use of essential oils. Smelling orange or any citrus essential oil will help shift the brain chemistry and knock out lower vibrational energies. Moving away from the location or situation and running cold water on your wrists may also help.

Symptoms of Psychic Attack:
- You sleep all night but wake up tired.
- Feel have a sense of a 'brain fog' that is hard to overcome.
- Constantly feel as if you are being watched.
- Unexplained bruises or scratches
- Buzzing or tingling
- Seeing silhouettes or shadows out of the corner of your eye.
- A constant, non-productive cough.

It seems everywhere we turn, there is someone offering advice on how to shield or protect ourselves from these elements. Often, we are told to "surround yourself in white light or put yourself in a bubble of white light. While this is generally good advice, let's look at the mechanics of these concepts and ask yourself, "How easy is it to pop a bubble?" and "If

I surround myself in white light, how long before it starts to dissipate?"

Use a tetrahedron. Geometrically speaking, a tetrahedron is the strongest shape we have. Replace that weak soap bubble of white light with the strength of a tetrahedron. A tetrahedron is a triangular pyramid with four triangular faces and a floor. Visualize yourself inside of this structure and clear yourself with white light. You can also bring up a violet flame, which will transmit the negative energy you release. This is a visualization technique, and it can take practice. View it as one of your most important spiritual practices. You can use this for yourself and your home.

There are many crystals out there, each type that vibrates with specific frequencies. When it comes to psychic protection, a couple of stones are tried and true. One is black tourmaline. You can keep small pieces in your pocket, purse, or even your child's backpack. Place larger pieces under your bed or at your front door entrance.

Elite Shungite is a bit newer and has some remarkable properties. It absorbs artificial energies, such as electronics and Wi-Fi. I have personally tested this with my Trifield Electromagnetic tester. When Elite Shungite is next to my cell phone or computer, the EMF numbers go down to zero. I purchased this (I make no commissions or earn referral fees). Go to Amazon and check out the Tri-Field EMF reader.

Take the time to meditate and ground yourself. When you do this, you literally pull yourself back to the center, which makes you stronger. You are also giving yourself the gift of time. We may only need a few minutes to meditate and get centered.

Our intuition is our most potent psychic ability. This cannot be emphasized enough. I know what you are thinking: seeing dead people is way sexier than working on building our intuition. In all seriousness, our intuition, when we listen to it, keeps us safe and guides us to make wiser decisions.

Utilizing our intuition keeps us safe; it's like an internal alarm system that we need to recognize. When someone rings our front doorbell, and we don't remember them, we go on high alert internally. You are using your intuition. Intuition should be applied to all aspects of our lives, including the unseen energetic forces.

Tuning into our gut instinct and using our inner guidance to navigate the elements of the unseen world enhances our "spidey senses" to better navigate the unseen, energetic world.

Our instinct is our innate reaction to a situation. Our intuition is our response to that innate reaction. When we learn to trust our instincts, our intuitive responses develop.

There is self-preservation and power in learning how to increase our psychic protection levels. It's always a constant work in progress. There is always something else to learn and enhance our auric fields.

CHAPTER 49

····✦✦✦····

ESSENTIAL OILS AND FREQUENCY: HOW ARE THEY CONNECTED?

*D*id you know that all humans and living things have a base frequency? The average healthy human frequency has been measured between 68 and 78MHz. When the measurement gets below 58MHz, disease sets in. Maintaining and creating a high frequency is key to longevity and good health. Essential oils carry very high frequencies that we can use to enhance and heal ourselves on many levels.

Frequency is simply vibration. The higher we can raise our base frequency, the stronger and healthier we are. Everything we surround ourselves with and even consume has frequencies attached to them. Living foods such as organic salads and fruits contain higher frequencies than processed foods that are prepacked and wrapped in plastics.

We live in a physical world where multitudes of frequencies surround us. Some frequencies are high; some are not. A

Japanese scientist, Dr. Masuro Emoto, led a series of experiments based on frequencies and what can lower or raise them. His work is still respected to this day. There is plenty of information on him on the internet, but his book captures most of what is out there.

Frequency is an unseen energy that can be measured using digital multimeters. Some, of course, are more accurate than others. Many individuals and institutions have measured essential oil frequencies.

All essential oils contain the life force energy of the plant from which they are derived. This means they all carry high frequencies, and each frequency carries different values. They can all be of assistance to

Essential oils can help us combat pain, heal, and even offer us psychic protection. They are all high-frequency and can aid us in a multitude of different ways.

Essential oils work not only on our physical bodies but also on our energetic bodies. They can help us in many ways. Our frequencies change all the time, and we also tend to absorb the frequencies around us. For example, have you ever missed a turn and gone to a new neighborhood that simply didn't feel good or right? There's a reason for that; it's a frequency differential.

We can use essential oils to help us shore up our baseline frequency. Frequency is energy, and energy knows no boundaries. The energetic signatures of essential oils go beyond their containers.

There are many essential oils we can use for a variety of situations. For example, if we are overridden with grief, lavender essential oil can be helpful. If we are feeling depressed, citrus oil can help to shift our mood. You can go on the internet and do your own research on how to use essential oils to help you through what you may be going through.

It's not about finding essential oils with the highest frequencies but rather those with the frequencies you need. For example, if you have a toothache, clove can help alleviate the pain more than another higher-frequency oil. Clove can also help remove toenail fungus. Frankincense oil doesn't do that, but it has anti-cancer properties.

There are many ways to use essential oils. One is to simply smell them. You can also buy a diffuser (make sure to get a decent one so it doesn't clog up and break). If using them directly on your skin, test a small area to ensure you don't have a skin sensitivity. People who have super light skin tones may be more sensitive to essential oils.

When the Christ child was born, the three Magi, or three magicians, knew he would be in for a wild ride on our beloved strife-ridden planet. Because of this, they gifted him three items: frankincense, gold, and myrrh. No one ever really asks the question as to why these three specific gifts. Gold makes sense, as it has a monetary value. But why essential oils and tree saps? Because they contain high frequencies. This is a form of psychic protection that Christ could use while walking on this earth plane.

Frankincense has a frequency of 147MHz, and myrrh has a frequency of 105MHz. When combined, these two essential oils work together, and their frequencies combined skyrocket, like 1+1=4.

Limiting them to three is challenging, as hundreds are out there! However, my all-time favorite is sacred frankincense.

There are three main varieties, each with different frequencies: Serrata, Carterii, and Sacra. I love the smell, and I use them in my spiritual toolbox all the time.

Orange essential oil is another one of my favorites; it is uplifting and can quickly remove brain fog.

Thieves oil. Since I am allergic to antibiotics, I use this to keep the wound clean when I cut myself. I also use it when I have a cold. I make a concoction of hot water with fresh lemon, local raw and unpasteurized honey, and 1-3 drops of Thieves oil. It helps combat the virus and soothe the throat.

Ok, I can't keep it to just three. It's kind of like asking me what my three favorite crystals are. I can't do that! But I use this trio when I have a sinus issue. Get hot water and 5-10 drops of clary sage essential oil, five drops of rosemary, and one drop of peppermint. Place your head over the bowl and a towel over your head and inhale briefly. Essential oils offer us so many natural remedies. All of what I have mentioned here is online in other places.

Ensure that any essential oils you purchase are 100% pure and that no additives or preservatives are in them. They are never needed. I prefer the Young Living brand. I am not an affiliate, but this is the group that I know and trust to give me good information: https://www.essentialhealthrn.com/

Bulgarian Rose essential oil has been touted as having the highest frequency and can be rather pricey, at around $1,000 an ounce. However, it smells good—way better than those fake rose perfumes out there. This oil has a frequency of 320MHz.

CHAPTER 50

···◆◆◆···

UNDERSTANDING TETRAHEDRON SACRED GEOMETRY & ITS POWER

*T*he tetrahedron is a sacred geometry shape and one of the five platonic solids, which are the core patterns of our physical creation.

A platonic solid is a geometrical shape with the same number of polygonal faces whose internal angles total 360 degrees. The requirement for platonic solids is that each of the faces is the same size, and when you add the angles, that total is 360 degrees. For this book, we are focusing only on the tetrahedron.

Sacred geometry is the belief that geometry and mathematical rations and proportions are found in music, nature, light, sound waves, and cosmology. Its origins trace back to ancient Egyptian and Mesopotamian cultures. Later, it reemerged in ancient Greece: think Pythagoras Theorem, for example. Platonic solids are found everywhere in nature and are the core basis of mathematics.

The tetrahedron is, geometrically speaking, the strongest shape we have. What makes it so remarkable is that each face is identical. Each face can be considered a base, as it has a four-way symmetry about it. This construct makes it a very valuable spiritual tool that we can all utilize.

The tetrahedron is a four-sided pyramid; no matter how you place it, it will always maintain stability and balance. The other platonic solids are easier to roll. This is an important concept to understand. It cannot be easily knocked over or broken.

The tetrahedron is linked to the element of fire, which is related to humanity's passion or drive. It is also related to the sun's power or light energy. The top of the tetrahedron can be considered an emitter of light or power. You can bring into the tetrahedron clearing energies, which are also healing energies. This is how the concept of healing works within the tetrahedron.

Visualizing or creating a tetrahedron in your spiritual practices can help you achieve balance and protection and envelope healing energies.

I utilize this sacred shape all the time. It can be used in many ways, one of which is through a visualization technique. Learning visualization techniques takes time and practice, so it's essential to give yourself time to learn this type of spiritual practice.

Buy and hold a small tetrahedron if you learn best through hands-on experience. Keep it with you. Close your eyes and imagine yourself holding that tetrahedron. Keep at it.

Next, you will learn how to 'see' the tetrahedron surrounding an object, such as a book or a flower—whatever works for you. Once you can visualize the tetrahedron surrounding the book, you can learn how to fill that space with white light, a healing energy.

Many spiritual practitioners will say things like, "Surround yourself with white light." Or "surround yourself in a bubble of white light for spiritual protection." Since energies have no boundaries, when we surround ourselves with white light, it takes a massive amount of effort. If you put yourself in a bubble of white light, well, bubbles are easy to pop. Why? Because they have no structure. If we take this same concept and visualize placing ourselves, even our living spaces, we can bring in a white healing Christ Consciousness light. This is a very powerful form of spiritual clearing and protection.

Another way to utilize the tetrahedron is to visualize it; you can create one with gold or any crystal. For example, if you are going through a heartbreak time in your life, imagine yourself inside a malachite or rose quartz tetrahedron.

If you need psychic protection, visualize yourself inside a double-walled tetrahedron. You can also request that angels from the higher realms and instruct them to remove all elements that are not for your greater good and to send them back to GodSource.

Bring the tetrahedron into your meditation practices. It will help you focus, clean, and clear your energetic fields, such as your aura. Give yourself the gift of time to add this to your spiritual toolbox. The tetrahedron is an asset to anyone's spiritual toolbox. Its basic construct makes it especially strong and durable.

CHAPTER 51

···✦·✦✦·✦···

WHAT IS MIRROR GAZING & IS IT DANGEROUS?

*M*irror gazing is a mediation technique for learning to see other dimensions. However, not all dimensions are safe, as many dark entities are lying in wait.

We are all multidimensional beings. We live a 3D, mortal life where we can see, touch, taste, smell… you get the idea. Mirrors are portals. Think about the movie Snow White and the phrase, "Mirror, mirror on the wall, who is the fairest of them all?" The wicked queen used the mirror as a portal to find information.

Mirror gazing goes way back to the Greeks, Egyptians, and many other cultures. It is associated with mystics, sooth-sayers, and seers. Mirror gazing can also be called scrying. The intent is to be able to communicate with 'spirits' or other dimensional entities.

Dr. Raymond Moody has re-popularized this paranor-mal technique to communicate with the dead primarily. Dr.

Moody is famous for his work with people who died and experienced an NDE (Near Death Experience). While the purpose of the NDE is to teach us all what happens upon death, there is still a lot to learn.

The issue with this is that when a person dies, we must ensure they cross over into the higher realms. My book, Soul Tribe: Navigating the Spiritual War, explains in greater detail what happens to the soul upon death and how you can help them.

Looking into a mirror and seeing how gorgeous you are is always a good thing. J Seriously, mirrors can become portals, and I am very hesitant to have anyone delve into this pseudoscience. If you decide to do so, please proceed with caution and wisdom.

When mirror gazing, expectations and what can happen can vary widely.

Is mirror gazing dangerous? Yes, it can be. Remember the movie The Conjuring? It is based on a true story that didn't end well. When a dark entity overpowers us, it can take possession of our bodies. What happens to the soul during this process? It is soul-napped and kidnapped but in another dimension.

Knowing and understanding what can happen is important when dabbling in spiritual practices. Mirror gazing, or scrying, is designed to communicate with other dimensional beings. Many times, there are dark entities who will join in and not have your greater good in mind. There may be shapeshifters or worse. Learning how to discern who or what you are communicating with is paramount to keeping your soul in a safe space.

When it comes to psychic abilities, people seem to want to see dead people for whatever reason that is exciting. The harsh reality is that a ghost soul is someone's loved one and needs help going Home.

There are countless spirits and entities; we must proceed with judicial caution when communicating with them. However, our intuition is our most valuable psychic ability. It's not as sexy as seeing dead people, angels, or demons, but our intuition keeps us safe and develops our wisdom.

Suppose you have a mirror in your home that you suspect is a portal. Some entities can come and go through it, but you can close it in several ways. Remember, the Light Side, those light beings that are a part of our spiritual team and higher, do not need to use mirrors or any other object to come into our home. Who does need this? Yep, the dark entities.

There are a few ways to close a mirror portal. One technique is to write the word "love" all over the back side of the mirror. The frequency and power of love do create a barrier to the dark side.

If the mirror has 90-degree angles, you can use a Sharpie pen and draw a small line in the corner to create a triangle, then color it in. The idea is your four-sided mirror, which now has eight sides and is the same shape as a protective bagua. This concept is derived from Chinese feng shui. The mirror then becomes a protective amulet.

Lastly, if you tried these techniques and that mirror is still an issue, you may need to remove the mirror and break it, then throw it away. Your spiritual safety is worth more than what any mirror costs. Do NOT donate a contaminated mirror to a charity or secondhand store. You do not want the karma of 'gifting' a mirror that is a portal to anyone.

Suppose you are thinking of learning more about mirror gazing or any other types of interdimensional activities. In that case, you need to learn how to discern who's who and what's what in these other dimensions. Spiritual safety is paramount. Mirror gazing and other such activities are not child's play.

CHAPTER 52

··· ✦ ✦ ✦ ···

DO DREAM CATCHERS
ACTUALLY WORK?

*D*reams are a large part of our spiritual experiences; not all dreams are for our greater good. Can a dream catcher help you with sleep, and how does it work? What are dream catchers? What do they do? How can I choose one that works for me?

Dream catchers are a Native American history from the Ojibwe and Lakota tribes. While these two cultures didn't mingle, they both had similar concepts when it came to dream catchers.

In Ojibwe lore, Asibikaashi, the spider woman, was their spiritual protector who protected the children from harm. As their tribe grew and traveled, she needed help protecting the children and made the women make dream catchers resembling a spiderweb. The dream catchers trapped bad dreams in the web while the good dreams floated down to the children.

The Lakota legend has dream catchers to trap the good ideas, dreams, and concepts to save them, and the negative ideas, bad dreams, and concepts pass through the center hole and dissipate.

The idea is that they are hung above the bed where someone is sleeping to catch dark dreams and energies before they can get into your energy field. The positive dreams and thoughts are allowed to stay.

The power of intention may also influence how a dream catcher works. For example, setting the intention that positive dreams and energies will only come to us in our sleep state can be beneficial.

Also, a dream catcher needs to be exposed to sunlight, as that is a clearing energy. If a dream catcher becomes full of negative energies, it will lose its effectiveness, just like any other physical object.

The purpose of the dream catcher is to protect us as we sleep. The Native Americans believed, and rightfully so, that the energies at night are calmer and make it easier for negative energies and entities to gain access to us, especially as we sleep.

Dream catchers may work better for some than others. This is true with all types of spiritual tools. Humans are not one size fits all. We carry different lineages, experiences, frequencies, and more within us.

If you have a history or a natural inclination towards Native American histories, maybe you have had past lifetimes, find yourself comfortable around talismans or other cultural aspects, you may discover dream catchers to feel at home, and they will work wonders for you.

Dream catchers have become popular in modern society as decorations. They appear in movies and television, such as The Vampire Diaries; the Twilight series even mentions dream catchers.

While dream catchers can be found in many spiritual stores, online, and other places, you must ensure that if you choose to get one, you learn how to feel its energy. As you look at it, does it bring you joy? Does it make you feel good? Do you feel neutral about it? Or you could pass by it to find another.

Choosing a dream catcher is a personal experience. What may be right for you may not be suitable for someone else. This is where the power of intuition can come in handy.

Dream Catchers have several components: the hoop, web (or weave), beads, gemstones, and feathers. They may contain all these elements or some of them. For example, some may have gemstones woven in, while others may not.

You want to look for dream catchers made by Native Americans and not manufactured in another country. Those that are handmade are the best option. They may be a bit more expensive, but you are also paying that person for their knowledge, creativity, and even energy that they infuse into them.

There are also many tutorials to teach you how to make your own. Once you learn, it may be a fun activity to bring supplies for your friends and family so that you can all make your own.

Dream catchers can be placed in bedrooms, above the bed, and even in the window. Ensuring your dream catcher can be cleared, sunlight is a good source for that.

As we embark on our spiritual paths, we must keep adding tools to our spiritual toolbox as we work on ascension and building our baseline frequencies.

CHAPTER 53

···✦✦✦···

WHAT IS REMOTE VIEWING?

R emote Viewing (RV) is the ability to project one's con-sciousness and subconscious to another time, space, and dimension. To better understand this concept, we need to understand that we are spiritual beings, way before we were ever human beings. Our souls have resided in spaces and places that were not on this earth.

Remote viewing is also considered a psychic skill, like clairvoyance. The concept of remote viewing transcends time, language, and culture. In ancient history, a remote viewer may have been called an "oracle." In more recent times, many governments have created remote viewing programs to defeat their enemies or to help find kidnapped persons.

Researchers made remote viewing more mainstream from the Stanford Research Institute with physicists Russell Targ and Harold Puthoff. Ingo Swann created this term.

Remote viewing is most often used to help find answers and solve problems. I have been able to use my remote viewing skills to 'see' what types of nefarious entities are harassing a client, and the most important aspect of this is to remove them properly. When I do this type of work, I view the fourth dimension remotely. Some call this limbo the lower astral or hells.

I have also been asked to locate missing persons on a few occasions. This is a different type of remote viewing, and I need to learn how to see what the missing person sees. Then, to make it a bit more complicated, I must figure out if the person is still alive.

The Three Main Types of Remote Viewing:

Associative Remote Viewing (ARV)

This type of remote viewing has become a methodology used to gain profits. The idea is that it is used to predict events, including stock market predictions, lottery numbers, and casino gaming. While this sounds fantastic, we must remember that this type of remote viewing may come at a karmic cost. If one manipulates futures for their benefit while exploiting others, there can be unforeseen consequences—karma always seeks balance.

Extended Remote Viewing (ERV)

Captain Skip Atwater originally coined the term Extended Remote Viewing. In this form of remote viewing, the viewer is put into a near theta state of relaxation and attended by an interviewer who directs and asks the viewer questions. Typically, this type of remote viewing takes longer, but the results may be more exacting.

Controlled Remote Viewing (CRV)

Controlled remote viewing is usually geography based. This type of remote viewing gained in popularity during the Cold War when the United States learned that Russia had remote viewing programs. CRV focuses on the physicality of objects and places. If you watched the movie Close Encounters of the Third Kind, there is a scene where Richard Dreyfus keeps getting these impulses or urges that he can't quite understand, and then he ends up building Devil's Tower (Wyoming) out of mashed potatoes. This movie explains how CRVs work, even with Hollywood-style embellishments.

Can anyone learn to become a remote viewer? It's a fair question to ask if anyone can become a remote viewer. Learning to RV is about building up your psychic skill sets. It's a spiritual practice that carries karmic implications. For example, I would never, ever remote view your home without your permission. That is a violation of your personal space. It's not much different than the concept of a home intruder entering your home and going through your possessions. To learn how to properly remote view, one needs to understand some basic tenets of spiritual law.

Remote viewing is like training for an athletic event. If you are a couch potato, I wouldn't recommend you sign up for the Ironman World Championship race next month. It would be best if you spent time training your body and mind for the event.

Many institutions offer remote viewing training, but I have yet to find any that provide spiritual protection practices.

When one is remote viewing, harmful unseen entities and energies can be picked up. This is because we are more than just human beings; we are spiritual beings.

I worked with a man who went to a remote viewing facility on the East Coast to learn how to remote view. When he returned, his five-year-old daughter became terrified and screamed "nothing." It turns out that dark entities flock to this facility to find their victims. After I worked with him and removed the dark entities, this became a distant memory for him and his daughter.

Sometimes, RV is learned innately, meaning it just happens naturally. When this is the case, chances are pretty good that this remote viewer has had RV experiences in their past lives. We all have heard of some anomaly where a three-year-old child can play the piano better than Mozart did. Why is this? Chances are that the soul's purpose is to excel in music, and they reincarnate with the same mindset over and over to become the best. Someone who has a natural remote viewing ability has done this before.

If you are interested in remote viewing, start by learning to listen and trust your intuition. Our intuition is our most powerful psychic ability. As we learn to develop our intuition, our natural psychic centers will open gradually if you are an impatient Aries, like me, learning to be patient in this process is critical.

When I work with a client, we work together as a team, and I do this by assisting the client with remote viewing. We learn to see the same elements so the client can see what is happening to them "behind the scenes," and we clean up the energies and entities. I work this way for a few reasons. One is that validation in the non-tangible world is essential, but it also assists the client on a deeper level.

CHAPTER 54

··· ◆ ◆ ◆ ···

WHAT IS ASTRAL PROJECTION?

*A*stral projection is the ability to separate the mind or con-sciousness from the body and to travel in different realms. When we leave our physical body, it is our soul energy that is traveling or experiencing elements that reside in other dimen-sions outside of the earth plane.

When we leave our physical body, it's important to note that our soul will always remain attached to the physical body through our aka cords, that elastic silvery blue cord that connects the soul energy to the physical body.

There are people out there who naturally soul travel and many who will learn how to do this. No matter which category you fall into, it's important to set intentions for safety and

The term astral refers to the nonphysical realms of exis-tence, where psychic and paranormal phenomena exist. A large part of these realms includes otherworldly beings and entities. It's important to note that not all these beings or enti-ties will have our greater good in mind.

Knowing that we are all spiritual beings having human experiences, it is a logical conclusion that astral projection is real.

When it comes to discussions around planes of existence, we need to take a hard look at the astral plane. This plane is also known as the fourth dimension and has been hijacked by nefarious entities that can only exist by utilizing our God-Source energy. These entities are where the concept of evil comes from. They are parasitic in nature and depend upon our suffering for their survival.

There are many other interdimensional planes of existence, and it is essential that we learn what they are and who or what resides there. Each plane of existence is built upon crystallized consciousness of a set of unique frequencies.

Astral projection happens when our soul leaves our physical bodies, and we travel to different planes of existence. Sometimes, this is where we learn lessons to help with our soul's purpose and growth. This may be where we meet up with our spiritual guides who help us navigate throughout our mortal lives. It can help us to shift our thoughts, beliefs, and expectations to help raise our frequency and states of consciousness. It's important to know that we need to use discernment when working in these realms. I will mention a few tools and strategies you can use to help ensure your soul is protected.

We need to understand that our souls are eternal. While we have all lived many lifetimes, we also exist between lifetimes. When we astral project or travel, we move about without the heaviness of the physical body. This can feel liberating for many. This may also explain the concept of flying dreams.

Is astral projection safe? Not always. I don't want to scare you, but this story is one of good intentions going bad. I worked with a man who paid a lot of money to go to a fancy, world-renowned institute to learn how to astral travel and remote view. He was there for two weeks, and he learned a lot. While at the institute, he began channeling his "guides" while astral traveling, and they were giving him all sorts of information. He felt fortunate and blessed to get these messages.

But the problems didn't unfold until he got home.

He continued astral traveling and gaining more information, but he soon found out he wasn't communicating with whom he thought he was. Suddenly, one night, his five-year-old daughter started screaming in her room, terrified. He saw the beings he was communicating with in the astral realms, which confused him about why his daughter would fear them. Her terror quickly grew to the point she could never be alone.

It turns out things were different from what they seemed. This being that he had been working with was a shapeshifter that followed him home and delighted in terrorizing his little girl. We were able to remove them from the home, and his daughter began to sleep in her own bed again.

Learning to vet and examine your situation is vital to ensure your safety. We do this all the time in our physical world.

Spiritual self-defense is a critical component in these realms. Here are a few recommendations to help keep you in a safer space.

Visualize yourself pouring salt over an entity whenever you communicate with an entity. Salt cleanses in all dimensions, and lower-frequency beings can't handle this very well.

When you go to sleep at night, put frankincense essential oil on your feet, solar plexus, and third eye. You can dilute it in a high-quality carrier oil to make it last longer. This is a huge frequency booster that can create a barrier of protection around you.

Visualize yourself in a tetrahedron, a four-sided pyramid. Fill it with white light. Many practitioners say to surround ourselves with a bubble of white light. Well, folks, all of us were children at one point, and we played with bubbles. Remember how easy they were to pop?

There are people for whom this is natural. If this is a natural process for you, it's still wise to learn to ensure your spiritual protection.

If you are unsure if you are astral projecting, these are some tips to get started. But first, as mentioned above, you must work on building your spiritual defense systems. The goal is to create and build healthy and strong soul energy.

Astral projection can help us understand that our souls are eternal. It's also possible to learn about your soul's history and gain insight into your soul's purposes. It can also help us raise our consciousness. Another benefit is learning how to sleep deeper and wake up with energy.

Tips for Learning How to Astral Travel:
Set your intention. Why do you want to do this? What do you hope to gain? Are you looking to learn more about your soul's purpose or to gain insights into a situation you are experiencing?

Work on relaxing your body. You can do this by lying down or sitting still—practice breathwork. A straightforward technique is inhaling slowly through the nose for two seconds and then slowly exhaling through the mouth for four seconds.

Focus on your body parts, starting with the feet and working up. You can add a mantra or intention statement while you do this.

Let your mind go. See where it takes you.

Journal your experiences. Simply free write and look for patterns as time goes on.

This is a spiritual practice, and it will take time to build up to the place where you want to be. Give yourself the gift of patience and be kind to yourself.

CHAPTER 55

·· ·◆ ◆ ◆ ·· ··

WHAT ARE THE DANGERS
OF LUCID DREAMING?

*I*s it dangerous to lucid dream? What is lucid dreaming? Do we all do it? Do some people have lucid dreams more than others? Is it possible to control lucid dreams?

Mainstream science tells us that lucid dreaming is a part of our sleep state when we are aware of what we are dreaming. These dreams are usually very vivid and may even have vibrant colors. Lucid dreaming usually happens during our REM state (Rapid Eye Movement), with faster breathing and heightened brain activity. Conventional science shows that our brain activity during lucid dreaming creates irregular brain patterns.

Is lucid dreaming more than meets the eye? I suspect that lucid dreaming is a hybrid form of our consciousness.

It's possible that lucid dreaming has more of a spiritual aspect than many scientists realize. When we sleep and dream lucid, we may leave our physical bodies.

There's a lot of information discussing lucid dreams' dangers. When we lucid dream, we may enter altered states of reality or other dimensions. Sometimes, when we are lucid dreaming, we are working, we visit with our deceased loved ones, and we can also work with our spirit guides.

There are also those of us who are actively engaged in battling a multidimensional spiritual war. There are some people, such as super soldiers, who are engaged in battle while they sleep. It's possible that they wake up with unexplained bruises, cuts, or bite marks. There are also some spiritually advanced people who have specific missions to remove nefarious entities that impact the earth plane. This type of lucid dreaming is not all that common, but I bring it up because it is essential.

One of the most significant issues with lucid dreaming is the disruption in our ability to get into a deep, theta state of sleep. This means we wake up not feeling rested, maybe even feeling anxious. If we lucid dream too often, this can start to impact our daily lives by making us chronically tired. This can cause us to engage in somewhat unhealthy habits, such as eating carbs and sugars to help stay awake and focused or needing a constant infusion of caffeine.

Constant lack of sleep will impact our mental health. Terrorists use sleep deprivation tactics for a reason. It's a form of psychological warfare. Sleep is critical to our overall health, mental, physical, and emotional. When we are tired, we react in a manner that may not be our norm.

Too much lucid dreaming may affect mental health. If the lucid dreams are negative or stressful, the emotions of the lucid dreams may stick with us. It may be an anxiety feeling we can't shake off. We can become preoccupied with our dreams, even to the point where we may become fearful of sleep.

Sometimes, a lucid dream feels so real that when we wake up, it takes us a moment to figure out where we are and what happened.

If the lucid dream is more of a nightmare, it can be highly stressful. If this is repeated, it adds to our emotional burden. If this happens, it would be worth learning some strategies to change the outcome of lucid dreams. The main physical impact of lucid dreaming is fatigue.

Those who experience lucid dreams may wake up feeling exhausted in the morning. You know you slept all night but can't explain why you are so tired.

If you lucid dream more than a few times per week, your sleep patterns could be altered. If this happens, you may need to work on strategies to retrain your ability to sleep soundly. Maybe it's playing music or turning off electronics a couple of hours before you go to bed.

To help you stay grounded and aware of your physical surroundings, you may want to sleep next to a small crystal or other object within your grasp.

If the lucid dream involves a fear, such as a snake, focus on an object that will remove that snake. This will give you your power back. You can then refocus and center yourself or even work on waking yourself up. Remind yourself that you are in control.

What connections do your lucid dreams make? Do they offer you a lesson or opportunity? We must remember that our minds are one of our most powerful assets. We can learn to control our dreams.

When it comes to lucid dreaming, we can learn a lot about ourselves. We can learn what triggers our fears and how to control the outcome. Learning to become in control of our dreams reduces our anxiety, helps us with problem-solving, and may increase our mental health and self-confidence.

If you find yourself lucid dreaming and the dreams feel negative, take the steps needed to control your dreams, learn from them, and move forward.

When you can control your dreams, you are creating your own virtual dreamscape—a dreamscape where you are in control of the outcome, a dreamscape that can be filled with beautiful colors and all those elements that make you feel at home. Perhaps it is a beach paradise, a meadow, or even a clean and fresh cityscape.

CHAPTER 56

··· ✦ ···

WHAT IS THE VIOLET FLAME &
HOW DOES IT AFFECT US?

*T*he violet flame is a spiritual tool that we can use to impact us as we navigate through life positively. We all have the ability within us to learn how to use and apply it. The violet flame is a subtle energy that we call on to clear ourselves and enable us to live a life of wisdom and discernment. It can also be used to help with subtle healing energies. This is a visualization practice.

The violet flame is a spiritual tool that transmutes negative energies to help clear your spaces. Do you remember the acronym ROY G BIV from school? This is the acronym for the color chart: red, orange, yellow, green, blue, indigo, and violet. Violet is the most energetic, and red is the least energetic. What is beyond violet is invisible to the naked eye. This is where the unseen energetic elements can impact us.

The violet flame is a spiritual tool that everyone needs in their toolbox. It helps to clean and clear our mind, body, and soul as we accumulate negative energies. We all accumulate negative energies as we navigate through life. We may visit a friend in a hospital, drive down the freeway, or go to school. These are normal mortal activities where we can collect negative energies.

The concept of alchemy is the ability to transform matter, and it is usually thought of in occult manners. The violet flame is said to have been a part of mystery schools and the occult. Saint Germain, an ascended master, is credited with bringing the violet flame back into modern times. He purports that this God-gifted spiritual tool helps to bring enlightenment and healing to humanity.

When we sit near a fire, the flames we see are its gaseous elements. When we can learn to control the flame, we control the fire, and when we control the fire, we control the outcome. The violet flame is a spiritual fire.

When we learn to utilize the violet flame, we gain the ability to transmute negative energies around us. This is because the frequency of the color violet has a higher intensity.

If you are new to the concept of the violet flame, start with mediation. If 'seeing' is difficult for you, use this image to study it and even stare at it. Learn how to draw this energy into your heart center and expand it throughout your entire body and even your home spaces.

The energy of the violet flame can heal us and clear the bonds of negativity. It can help us to shift our negativity and clear it. When we meditate using the violet flame, it promotes universal love and healing to ourselves and all that we encounter.

When we can learn tools to help us on our spiritual path, the violet flame is essential. It helps us to connect to God, shift negative energy into positive energy, and can even help us with spiritual healing.

Regular use of the violet flame will help with improving one's frequency.

We all need to grow our spiritual toolboxes, and adding the violet flame to yours will help you develop your spiritual awareness. The violet flame may be one of our most underutilized resources. Learn to use it and develop your skills in the power of the violet flame.

Many adepts, saints, spiritual practitioners, sages, shamans, and others have used the violet flame. However, it is not limited to those with titles. It is a tool available to everyone: the more people who know how to use it, the cleaner and clearer the planet.

The color violet is a highly spiritual energy, and we are spiritual beings. The crown chakra is a violet color, and this is the chakra that connects us to the Divine.

When we are engaged in energy healing, we are involved in the inner work and healing of the soul. The violet flame is a tool of our mind. Our mind is the most powerful asset we can utilize beyond time and space. It may sound complex and complicated, but bear with me. Close your eyes and visualize the color violet in front of you; this is easier for some than others, and that is ok (spirituality is never a contest). Once you have that now, try to make that energetic color flow. Spend some time practicing. After all, this is a spiritual practice.

When we commit to doing that inner work and forego spiritual bypassing, amazing things can happen. Using the violet flame can immensely assist us in transmuting old patterns, finding true joy, and being actively engaged in our spiritual healing and development.

When I work with clients, I often use the violet flame to clear our space before we begin, during the session to vet what we are dealing with, and even at the end, to clean up the spaces, ensuring nothing was left behind.

One of the best websites to learn about Violet Flame and how to use it is Violetflame.com.

ACKNOWLEDGMENTS

I need to thank God and my amazing spiritual team for all their help and support over many lifetimes. For without them, I would be lost. Thank you all for sticking by me even when I have been super angry and frustrated at you all, especially during those dark and challenging times.

To my family, I would not be the person I am today without them. We have not had a traditional life by any means. But knowing that we have each other always will bring me a sense of peace and unconditional love. We have and always will love each other. My love for you is intense and powerful.

Now and then, we are blessed with a friend who truly understands us and knows what we need. Thank you, CS, for being that person for me and for constantly pushing me forward.

ABOUT THE AUTHOR

A Remote Viewer, Author, and Speaker, Laura Van Tyne holds a B.S. in Education, a B.A. in Spanish, and a Master's degree in Second Language Acquisition, with much of her life spent as a middle school teacher.

Twenty years ago, the paranormal realm broke through her home, and she stopped teaching to determine how to keep her family safe. Today, she helps others with similar problems when faced with the unseen world.

Laura focuses on soul health and how we can create a healthy soul. The unseen, energetic world impacts soul health and mitigates our free will. When we learn to discern other-worldly beings—who they are and where they come from—we take our power back. And when we learn to connect with light beings, we can attain wisdom, insight, and fantastic assistance along our karmic journey.

Reincarnation is a part of our soul experiences. We all die. However, we rarely discuss what to do upon death. That is the key to soul health, wellness, and sovereignty.

Laura specializes in Past Life Regression, Etheric Implant Removal, Quantum Healing Hypnosis, MILAB Abduction, Soul Integration, and Spiritual Self-Defense.

For more information about how to work with Laura, online programs, speaking engagements, and additional services, visit thekarmicpath.com

Made in United States
North Haven, CT
09 October 2024

58531124R00189